INTEGRATED RURAL DEVELOPMENT PROGRAMME

About the Author

R.K. MAHAJAN (*b*. 1953) received his M.A. and Ph.D. in Economics from the University of Jammu, Jammu. He received Gold Medal for standing first in M.A. Economics.

At present, Dr. Mahajan is teaching M.A. and M.Phil. and guiding research in the P.G. Department of Economics, Punjabi University Regional Centre, Bhatinda. Prior to that he was with the teaching faculties of Department of Economics, University of Jammu, Jammu and D.A.V. College, Malout (Punjab).

His areas of interest are Agricultural and Rural Economics. He has been actively engaged in research in these fields. He co-authored a a book, "***Technological Change and Agricultural Development in India***". He supervised a ICSSR-sponsored research project, "***Impact of New Agricultural Strategy in Jammu & Kashmir***". He was Project Director of a recently completed ICSSR-sponsored research project, "***Differential Gains of IRDP in Punjab***". He has many research papers to his credit published in leading journals of India. He is a member of P.G. Board of Studies in Economics, Faculty of Arts and Social Sciences and M.Phil. Course Committee in Economics of Punjabi University, Patiala. He is a member of many academic bodies in the field of Economics at the national level.

INTEGRATED RURAL DEVELOPMENT PROGRAMME

(A Study of Problems and Prospects in Punjab)

R.K. MAHAJAN

CONCEPT PUBLISHING COMPANY PVT. LTD.
NEW DELHI-110059

The Indian Council of Social Science Research gave the financial support towards the publication of this work. However, the responsibility for the contents of the book- facts, opinions, conclusions, etc, - is entirely that of the author and not of the ICSSR.

ISBN: 978-81-7022-333-7

First Published 1991

Published and Printed by

Concept
Since 1974

Concept Publishing Company Pvt. Ltd.
A/15-16, Commercial Block, Mohan Garden,
New Delhi-110059 (India)
T: 91-11-41101460
E: publishing@conceptpub.com, *W*: www.conceptpub.com

PREFACE

RURAL DEVELOPMENT Programmes are expected to serve a broad set of objectives such as a direct attack on poverty, increasing the productivity of the poor, self-help and grass-root participation, uplifting the rural poor from abysmal poverty etc. Gunnar Myrdal states that rural development embraces everything done to improve condition in the villages including the sponsoring of co-operatives; in a sense it encompasses all the policy efforts directed towards rural uplift. The accent of the programme remains on multi-purpose approach, self-help, people's participation and technical and material assistance. A number of programmes have been adopted by the States in India for improving the quality of life in the rural areas for past forty years. In the early years of planning, Community Development Programme (1952) was initiated to bring about a desired qualitative change in rural areas through peoples' participation. Later on, a number of programmes viz., Intensive Agricultural District Programme (IADP) (1960-61), High Yielding Variety Programme (HYVP) (1965-66), Small Farmers Development Agency (SFDA) and Marginal Farmers and Agricultural Labourers Agency (MFALA) (1971), Drought Prone Area Programme (DPAP) (1975) etc., were brought into operation to usher in the development of agriculture, backward areas and weaker sections in the rural areas. The stress in these programmes shifted from agricultural development to area development to target group development to direct attack on poverty.

It is now generally agreed that rural development strategies of 1950s and 1960s have not benefited the small farmers and agricultural labourers. No doubt, during this period, the general conditions of the rural areas improved, but the down trend in poverty was slow and economic inequalities were accentuated. Even the special programmes initiated in 1970s for the small farmers, marginal farmers and agricultural labourers could not do much help to mitigate rural poverty and lessen economic inequalities. The chapter on 'Survey of Rural

Development Programmes' studies the rural development thinking, organisation, achievements and failures of the rural development programmes started for the past four decades.

Poverty is rural based. The efforts should be made to know the incidence of rural poverty. It is felt that during the period of rapid agricultural growth, the share of the poorer section in aggregate income and consumption has not improved. The real wages show a constant decline particularly during 1970s. The assets with rural poor people are meagre to raise their standard of living. The chapter on 'Differential Rural Scenario' explains the intensity of the problems of rural poverty, inequalities and 'trickle down' of benefits of the rural development programmes.

Integrated Rural Development Programme (IRDP) is one of the biggest programmes of poverty alleviation package which is now in operation in our country. The success of the programme lies in properly identifying beneficiaries and providing income generating assets to ensure continued employment and income for them. While IRDP is well conceived for improving the quality of life in the rural areas, its implementation has not been proper and according to the set guidelines. A number of families are still to feel its impact. Its gains are not equally distributed among the different sections of the rural society. Therefore, the questions arise: How many deserving poor receives the benefit of IRDP? What kind of assets are they provided with? Have the income generating assets sponsored under IRDP diversified the rural economy? What is the status of assets with the beneficiaries? How much are the gains of IRDP in terms of assets, income, consumption and employment? What proportion of beneficiaries cross the poverty line? How far the gains of IRDP are equally distributed among the different sections of the rural society? The present study tries to answer some of these questions with the help of both primary and secondary data.

India is a vast country with heterogeneous agroclimatic regions, diverse administrative set-ups and social groups. Therefore, it is better to undertake a study in a State or region, because a State or region is usually far more homogeneous than the country. The present study investigates and evaluate the IRDP in Punjab.

This study has been financed by the Indian Council of Social Science Research (ICSSR), New Delhi. Without the Council's active and adequate financial support, this study could hardly be under-taken. I am immensely grateful to the ICSSR for this help. Any how, the

Council is not responsible for the analysis I have done or the conclusions I have arrived at.

I am thankful to the consultant of ICSSR, Dr. S.S. Johl, Chairman, Commission for Agricultural Costs and Prices and former Vice-Chancellor, Punjabi University, Patiala for his valuable suggestions. I am highly benefited from the same.

I take it my privilege to express my deepest gratitude to Dr. H.K. Manmohan Singh, Vice-Chancellor, Punjabi University, Patiala for his encouragement and help.

During the course of study I am highly benefited from the discussion with Prof. (Dr.) A.N. Sadhu, Director, Rural Development, IMPA, Sri Nagar, Prof. (Dr.) G.K. Chadha, CSRD, JNU, New Delhi, Dr. C.S. Nagpal, Director, PURC, Bhatinda, Dr. S.K. Gupta, Punjabi University, Patiala and Principal S.C. Khosla, D.A.V. College, Malout. I pay my debt of gratitude to them. My thanks are due to my friends Dr. Iqbal Singh, Sh. S.R. Jhamb and Dr. Satnam Singh. The library staff of Punjabi University, Regional Centre, Bhatinda, D.A.V. College, Malout and JNU, New Delhi were very co-operative and kind to me. The BDOs of different blocks, Bank Personnels, Panchayat Members and respondents were kind enough in answering my queries.

The book would not have been possible but for the constant encouragement, patience and sacrifices rendered by my wife, Reeta.

I would also like to thank my publishers for their co-operation in seeing the book through the press and for expediting the publication of the book.

R.K. MAHAJAN

Punjabi University
Regional Centre
Bhatinda

CONTENTS

LIST OF FIGURES

LIST OF TABLES

INTRODUCTION

ONE OF the major objectives of national economic policy, ever since India adopted planning, has been the development of rural sector. Although the approach, contents and methodology of the programmes have undergone numerous changes during the past more than four decades, yet the problem of improving the lot of rural poor has been the basic theme of rural development strategies. In the early years of planning, Community Development Programme (1952) was initiated to bring about a desired qualitative change in rural areas through peoples' participation. Later on, a number of programmes viz. Intensive Agricultural District Programme (1960-61), High Yielding Variety Programme (1965-66), Small Farmers Development Agency and Marginal Farmers and Agricultural Labourers Agency (1971), Drought Prone Area Programme (1975), Integrated Rural Development Programme (1980) etc. were started in the country.

The programmes of rural development initiated in 1950s created the basic infrastructure needed for rural areas. In 1960s the main objective of rural development programmes was to achieve rapid growth in agriculture through intensive cultivation. These programmes have resulted into Green Revolution and food self-sufficiency for India. But, it is now generally agreed that the income inequalities have further increased by these programmes. For example, the Gini ratio for household incomes increased from 0.34 in 1953-54 to 0.48 in 1967-68. Rural poverty (based on Rs. 16 per capita per month in 1960-61 prices) in rural Punjab, heartland of green revolution, increased from 10 per cent in 1960-61 to 23 per cent in 1970-71. There was a general neglect of small farmers and agricultural labourers. They could not benefit in proportion either to their numbers or to their needs from the various programmes of rural development during 1950s and 1960s. Most of the programmes implemented in 1970s and 1980s aimed at to achieve growth with equity in the rural areas. Thus, the rural development programmes implemented in the rural areas created infrastructure, relieved the country from the food problem and brought general improvement in the living condition of the rural population. Now a large number of children in the rural areas have started going to schools, more and more villages are getting electrified, essential medical facilities are accessible, which clearly indicate that the general economic condition in the rural areas have improved.[1]

Despite the over-all progress in rural areas, the incidence of poverty continues unabated. In 1960-61, the number of people living below poverty line in India was 202 million (56.8 per cent of total population) which rose to 282 million (41.50 per cent of total population) in 1981-82.[2] A review of past development programmes revealed that the country was nowhere near the eradication of poverty.

The land distribution pattern is still skewed towards large farmers. This point can be supported by giving NSS data . As per the 8th round of NSS (1953-54), about 74 per cent of ownership holdings of the size group of two hectares and less covered only around 17 per cent of the owned area. There was a marginal improvement in this position in 1960-61, for example, according to 17th round of NSS (1960-61), the corresponding figures were 72 per cent and 20 per cent, respectively. On the other hand, about 3 per cent of the size group 12 hectares and more accounted for 28 per cent of the owned area and corresponding figures in 17th round were 2 per cent and 23 per cent, respectively. In 26th round (1970-71), 78 per cent holdings of size two hectares or less owned 24 per cent of the area against which 0.4 per cent holdings of size 12 hectares and above had 8 per cent of the area. The pattern of distribution of operational holdings was also not far too different from the ownership holdings.

As a result rural development programmes which put more stress on the development of agriculture, benefited those who had viable holdings and adequate resources. There was a weak trickle down of the growth of agriculture to the unprivileged sections of the society.

Since a majority of rural households have either limited or no access to productive agricultural land, these programmes were insufficient to reduce poverty. Francis Frankel found that the majority of farmers in the areas where Green Revolution shaped well experienced a relative decline in their economic position and the share croppers cultivating on oral lease suffered an absolute deterioration in their living standard.[3] Moreover, these programmes started with the hope that the rapid agricultural development benefiting a few would 'trickle down'. But this idea nearly proved to be false. Consequently, inequalities in the flow of benefits resulted from these programmes.

During Fourth and Fifth Plans certain programmes, viz., Small Farmers Development Agency (SFDA), Marginal Farmers and Agricultural Labourers Agency (MFALA), Drought Prone Area Programme (DPAP) etc. were implemented in a number of blocks in the country for disadvantaged people and depressed areas. These programmes emphasised not only raising the agricultural output but also generating employment through subsidiary occupations. However, the programmes could not continue at the targeted pace and they could utilise only half of their outlay during first five years of operation.[4] The number of agricultural labourers, marginal and small farmers who derived benefits from these programmes were also very small. There was, therefore, a need to call for a bigger programme to remove the degrading form of rural poverty.

The drafts of Sixth (1978-83 and 1980-85) and Seventh (1985-90) Plans placed greater emphasis on alleviation of rural poverty. The Sixth Plan asserted 'so far it has not been possible to make a dent on poverty on account of the inadequate rate of growth of the economy, uneven distribution of income and consumption as well as high rate of growth of population. The reduction in poverty should, therefore, receive the highest priority in our development strategy'.[5] For this, Integrated Rural Development Programme (IRDP) has been initiated as a strategy of direct attack on rural poverty. Draft Seventh Plan justifies the continuation of the programme on account of insufficient percolation of benefits to the poor from overall economic growth.

As a major poverty alleviation programme the IRD programme provides assistance to target groups of small and marginal farmers, agricultural labourers and rural artisans. It provides assistance to target families for purchasing productive assets and enables them to improve their standard of living and skip over poverty line. The District Rural Development Agencies (DRDA) and Development Blocks have been implementing the programme at the district and block level. The programme is in operation in all the Development Blocks (5011) of the country now.

The main objective of the IRD programme is to transfer productive assets to below poverty line households, identified in advance, for self-employment and for raising their income. The main thrust of the programme is on developing (i) *primary sector* i.e. programmes for agriculture, animal husbandry, fisheries etc.; (ii) *secondary sector* i.e.

programmes for village and cottage industries, skill formation and supporting services; and (iii) *tertiary sector* i.e. organised marketing, processing and allied activities. Unlike the earlier programmes of rural development, IRD programme is far beyond land-based activities and includes secondary and tertiary sectors with emphasis on formation of new skills for self-employment.

Some of the recent studies point to the weaknesses in the implementation of the IRD programme and its little impact on weaker sections. Most of these studies are based on first a few years of the introduction of the programme. However, a review of these studies will throw light on the working of the programme.

The Programme Evaluation Organisation (PEO)[6] of the Planning Commission, New Delhi, in its evaluation study report on IRDP for 1983-84 based on 16 States, reveals that about 88 per cent of 1163 selected beneficiary households reported an increase in their income, 77 per cent acknowledged an increase in their consumption level, 37 per cent of the reported households realised increase in their family assets after adoption of IRD programme. This study also reported misclassification of rural poor. About 26 per cent of the total selected beneficiaries were already having higher annual income than the prescribed limit of Rs. 3,500 for a target family. This study is comprehensive but it is difficult to segregate the problems of implementation and impact of the programme in the individual states as they widely differ in socio-economic, political and climatic terms. Therefore, a micro level study of an individual State or a district can throw a better light on the working of the programme.

In U.P., Balishter (1986)[7] reported that financial assistance given to the poor families had marginal impact on income of the beneficiaries in Agra district. According to him only 23 per cent of eligible beneficiary families were able to cross the poverty line. The eligible landless beneficiaries could cross the poverty line in a larger number than the small and marginal farmers. It is found that the main defect of this study is that it is based on only one financial institution, i.e., State Bank of India, Agra.

In a case study of IRDP in a Kerala village, Krishanan (1985)[8] concluded that majority of the beneficiaries to the extent of 80 per cent (based on annual family income of Rs. 3500) and 63.25 per cent (based on monthly per capita income of less than Rs. 76) were not eligible for assistance under the programme.

A study[9] was conducted by State Bank of Bikaner and Jaipur in

1984 in Bikaner district regarding the impact of IRDP on selected beneficiaries. It showed that most of the beneficiaries, particularly landless, had acquired camel carts, cows or buffaloes or sheep and goats. However, a large percentage of these beneficiaries were without the assets at the time of survey. Similar conclusions were also drawn by many other studies.[10]

A number of studies reported that majority of the beneficiaries were not able to cross poverty line. The NABARD (1984)[11] survey reveals that the percentage of beneficiaries whose income had risen above poverty line of Rs. 3,500 worked out to 40 per cent of total beneficiaries. These figures would have been much smaller than as reported in the survey if the minimum level of income had been adjusted to inflation after adoption of the programme.

Prof. Rath[12] raised doubts about the poverty eradication character of IRD programme. The main theme of his paper is that IRDP, based on distribution of assets to the poor for creating self-employment, is not going to remove poverty or help in the creation of wage employment. His criticism of the programme is based on the fact that the risk bearing and management capacity of poor households is extremely limited to make self-employment ventures a success. The subsidy element has encouraged corruption in rural areas and has raised indebtedness in many cases. There has been poor percolation of gains. His estimate, on the basis of NABARD study, is that about 18.7 per cent of the total beneficiaries might have crossed the poverty line.

Integrated Rural Development Programme is widely publicised programme which attracted the maximum public and Government attention as a programme of achieving egalitarian socio-economic distribution. Summing up the criticism levelled against IRDP by different studies, N.J. Kurian attacks the basic philosophy of the programme, its economic rationality and its viability.[13] 'It is argued that even if the programme is implemented as planned, without any malpractices or leakages, the benefits to the poor may not be significant or sustainable. A good part of what is given to the poor through IRDP will be taken away, through the social process and market operations by the rich and powerful'. He also quoted a study of Prof. Dantwala on the same line of thinking. Equity-oriented policies and programmes pursued within the cast iron inequitous economic structure — of ownership of assets will not only be sell-defeating, but may prove counter productive through a 'trickle up'. More simply, a direct attack on poverty without an equally direct attack on the structure, which has bred poverty and continues to do so, is an illusion at best, fraud at worst. Some critics of the programme lay emphasis on wage employment over asset distribution to the beneficiaries.

One thing, however, becomes very clear that rural development is still a very serious issue with the planners of the country and more has to be done than what have been done in the past 40 years. Giving a buffalo or a sewing machine or public loan in full view of camera to a target household will not make him rich. The prevalent practice of formulating the development programmes from above and thrusting upon the target households without caring for their perceptions will not make them people programmes but Government programmes.

The main objective of this study is not to discuss the philosophy of rural development programmes but focus attention on distributional gains of rural development programmes especially IRD programme on various sections of rural people. In this study, the following questions are raised:

(a) What is the economic performance of different rural development programmes in the study area?
(b) Which section of the society is able to derive maximum benefit?
(c) How far IRDP is successful?
(d) How are the gains regarding income, consumption and assets from IRDP distributed among different sections of the society?
(e) What are the main problems in the implementation of the programme?

These and similar other questions are raised in this study.

This study is based on the secondary and primary data collected by the researcher from sampled beneficiaries in the study area. The study is located in Punjab. The present study is divided into seven chapters. Second chapter discusses the philosophy, implementation and economic performance of rural development programmes in the Punjab. Third chapter gives the position of weaker sections *vis-a-vis* better-off people in the rural Punjab. Fourth chapter appraises the Integrated Rural Development Programme. Fifth chapter explains the differential gains of IRDP to the beneficiaries. This chapter is based upon the empirical data. Sixth chapter spells out the problems and prospects of IRDP in Punjab. In the end, summary and conclusions of this study are given.

NOTES

1. Prof. Raj Krishna, "The Crucial Phase of Rural Development", *Kurukshetra*, November 1, 1979, p. 11.
2. *Source:* Annual Report, 1985-86, Govt. of India, Deptt. of Rural Development, New Delhi, and K. Sundhram and Suresh D. Tendulkar, "Poverty in the mid-term Appraisal", *EPW*, XVIII, Nos. 45 & 46, November 5-15, 1985.
3. Sachchidananda, "Strategies of Rural Development in India: A Search for Alternatives", in *Rural Development in South Asia* (ed.) by L.P. Vidyarthi, 1982, Concept Publishing Co., New Delhi.
4. Sarathi Acharya & Satish Jha, "Rural Development Efforts in India : An Assessment". *Productivity*, January-March 1979, pp. 487-502.
5. Buta Singh, "Policy Options for Poverty Alleviation", *Kurukshetra*, November, 1984, p. 4.
6. Evaluation Study Report on IRDP for 1983-84. The Programme Evaluation Organisation, Planning Commission, New Delhi.
7. Dr. Balishter, ". . . . and find out what ails IRDP", *Yojna*, May 16-31, 1986, pp. 20 to 22.
8. A.C. Kutty Krishanan, "A Case Study of IRDP in a Kerala village", *IJAE*, Vol. XXXIX, No. 3, July-September 1985, pp. 259-265.
9. State Bank of Bikaner and Jaipur, Evaluation Study of the beneficiaries in Bikaner, Jaipur, 1984.
10. (a) A.S. Guleria *et al.*, "Strategy for the effectiveness of Animal Husbandry Schemes within IRDP", *IJAE* Vol. XLI No. 4, Conf. No., October-December, 1986.

    (b) Ahuja, Kanta & Bhargava, IRDP – an evaluation, *Jaipur Institute of Development Studies, Jaipur*, 1984.
11. NABARD, Study of Implementation of IRDP (memo), Bombay, 1984.
12. Nilkantha Rath, "Garibi Hatao — Can IRDP Do It?" February, 1985, pp. 238-246.
13. N.J. Kurian, 'IRDP : How Relevant is it'? *EPW*, December 26, 1987, A161-A174.

TWO

SURVEY OF RURAL DEVELOPMENT PROGRAMMES

FOR OVER four decades the planners of India are striving for achieving higher stages of development and self-reliance in the economy and to provide the basic necessities to the weaker sections of society. Policy-makers and planners have been emphasising the need for transforming rural areas where about 70 per cent of the population live. A number of rural development programmes have been started for the last more than 40 years in order to realise the desired goals. The approach has been ranging from Community Development to agricultural development and to direct attack on the rural poverty of the target groups. Despite some success of these development programmes, the problems of rural poverty and unemployment are unabated and continue to draw the attention of our policy-makers and planners.

The Punjab is a leading State of Indian union. The economic position of the people of the Punjab is better than any other State. This State led the green revolution. The poverty is the lowest in the State. But even then there is a need to improve the economic condition of those households which are below poverty line. The State adopted the various programmes for rural development time-to-time for the agricultural development and welfare of the weaker sections. This chapter examines the different programmes of rural reconstruction and development schemes in the rural Punjab since Independence. This historical analysis has two main objectives:

1. it will indicate the activities undertaken and character of organisational structures used by the various programmes;
2. it will try to evaluate the programmes of rural development in the State.

We shall discuss the objectives and underlying assumptions as well as content and adequacy of the programmes started after Independence. Most of the data used in this study are based on secondary sources, e.g., planning drafts, Annual Plans, Statistical Abstracts, Administrative and official reports etc.

Community Development Programmes (CDP)

The community development programmes were launched in early fifties in Punjab. Before these programmes, the concerned departments were carrying out their activities in the rural areas through their own functionaries at the State, district and village levels independently without any co-ordination. These departments were able to carry on some minimum development works touching a few aspects, covering only certain sections of the rural people. It has been observed that vocal and influential people mainly benefited from those development activities.[1] In other words, the development activities started by the different departments were segmented, disintegrated and benefiting only privileged section of the society.

The official CDP was introduced in October 1952. The basic objective of the programme was to serve the rural people and reach maximum of them. This programme aimed at the total development of the rural people, to increase production through the application of scientific technology, as well as better utilisation of man power and the extension of the principle of co-operation. In this programme, community development was regarded as the method and the National Extension Service (NES) as the agency for the socio-economic transformation of rural society.[2] It was considered that rural life is an organic whole and no improvement in any part is possible unless a concerted effort is made in all sectors of the economy simultaneously. Therefore, the programme covered a wide range of activities, viz. agriculture, animal husbandry, irrigation, co-operation, village and small-scale industries, health and sanitation, education, communication and housing etc.

The basic principles[3] underlying the CDP were that:

(i) the motive force for improvement should come from the people themselves. Vast unutilised energy lying dorment in the country side should be harnessed for constructive work for the benefit of the community as a whole;

(ii) the co-operative principles should be applied in its infinitely varying forms, for solving all problems of rural life; and

(iii) organised efforts for agricultural development and to construct works of common benefit to the community such as the village roads, tanks, school buildings, health centres, pavement of streets, construction of *pucca* drains etc. should be made. An awakening amongst the people was to be created for improving their social economic condition.

The objectives and strategy of CDP were changed many a times after its inception in 1952. In the beginning the community development programmes were used to increase agricultural production. The key projects promoted by the Government for the development of agriculture included land reforms, i.e., land tenure reforms, ceiling on land, the consolidation of land holdings, the establishment of new regulated markets for disposing of the farm produce etc. In the beginning of Second Five Year Plan, the emphasis of the programme shifted to industrialisation in which diversified agriculture was to play a complementary role.

The programme was implemented through "Development Blocks". The block was made the unit for rural development. The whole State was divided into 116 development blocks. Each block consisted of about 100 villages covering the population of 60 thousand to one lakh. The block was headed by Block Development Officer (BDO). BDO was under the State Development Department, but was operationally answerable to the Deputy Commissioner of the District. His main function was to co-ordinate the activities of the officers of the various departments engaged in rural development work at the block level such as agriculture, education, public health, co-operatives, rural industries department etc. These officials were called as Extension Officers (EOs). The EOs were to work as supervisors for the Village Level Workers (VLWs) as well as to assist the BDO. The EOs were subject to dual control; operationally they were controlled by the BDOs, but their technical control was vested with their department officer at the district level.

At the bottom level, the village units were served by village level workers. Each block was provided with a team of 10 VLWs. The VLW was a multi-purpose functionary. He was happened to be a single representative of all departments, which were linked with rural development programmes. Increase in agricultural production could only be achieved with the most intensive efforts that could be organised at the village level through VLW for:[4]

(i) full utilisation of irrigation facilities, including maintenance/repairs of field channels and community irrigation works, etc.,
(ii) distribution of improved seeds to all the cultivators,
(iii) increase in the area under multiple cropping,
(iv) installation of new minor irrigation works,
(v) development of poultry, fishery and dairy products,
(vi) adoption of improved agricultural practices such as soil conservation, dry farming, drainage, and soil reclamation etc., and
(vii) introduction of improved agricultural implements.

In Punjab, there was a mixed response to this programme. The programme is evaluated in the subsequent paragraphs. The data used for the years before 1966 included Haryana also. There were 229 blocks prior to re-organisation of Punjab in 1966. At the end of the First Plan, 60 blocks were covered under the programme. By the end of Second Five-Year Plan, the CDP covered 20,236 villages and a population of 103.6 lakh. With the opening of 57 new blocks during the Third Five-Year Plan, the entire composite State was covered under the Community Development and National Extension Service Programmes.

Community Development Programme increased the production of foodgrains considerably. At the time of Independence the agriculture of Indian Punjab was subsistence type. It had to import foodgrains to the extent of 75,000 tons.[5] So it was a food deficit State at the time of independence. The index of production of total foodgrains increased from 100 in 1950-51 to 114 in 1955-56 and 160 in 1960-61. The compound growth rate of total foodgrains was 4.37 per cent per year during 1950-60. The share of the agricultural sector in the total income of the State also increased from Rs. 292 crores in 1952-53 to Rs. 360 crores in 1959-60. The most important achievement of the programme was construction of 6700 miles of *kachcha* roads to connect the villages with main roads in the marketing centres and pavement of 20 lakh square yards of streets.

During the Third Plan, 108 thousand irrigation wells, 4.2 thousand pumping sets and 2.5 thousand tube-wells were installed in the State.

In addition, under the health and sanitation programme, 4.3 thousand drinking wells were sunk, 12.2 thousand old wells were renovated, and 43.1 thousand pumps were installed. About 13 thousand kilometres of *kachcha* roads were constructed.[6]

Despite the achievements of the programmes, it could not bring about the desirable results in increasing the agricultural production, removing illiteracy, improving the health and hygiene etc. There may be a number of reasons for the same. Prof. S.C. Dube points out that CDP emphasised cultural goals rather than output goals. There was a great deal of high minded talks and relatively little purposive action.[7] The Punjab as well as the whole country was under the severe grip of food crisis. There were recurring problems of drought and famine. But this programme neither made the significant contribution to agricultural production nor effectively handled the problems of drought and famine. There was lack of inter-departmental co-ordination. Many a times, more than one department was engaged for the implementation of a single programme.

The officials handling the various programmes were themselves not clear about the objectives and strategies of the programme. They were also not trained to take this gigantic task. The report[8] of the State Evaluation Committee on the working of the Community Development Programme found the Department deficient on almost every count; poorly selected personnel without proper training serving time; hierachical attitudes, insufficient attention to rewards for good people; lack of effective interest on the part of those incharge; non-co-operation by the State departments responsible for development work with the community projects; ineffectiveness in motivating the farmer with a desire to progress in making him self-reliant and in filling staff positions.[9]

The evaluation of the programme shows that the most of the benefits of the programme had gone to the privileged section of the rural society — landlords, moneylenders, big farmers etc. — and the weaker sections received only the normal benefits. Thus the CDP enriched the few and could not enhance the cause of social justice.

There was a lack of co-ordination between the departments at the State level, among the officers at the district level and block level. The administrative powers were also concentrated in the hands of the senior officers. This lack of co-ordination and concentration of administrative powers led to avoidable delays in the execution of community development projects and resulted in the dilution of responsibility. A long chain of intermediary officers between the sanctioning authority and the executing officials at the grass-roots made it difficult to ensure timely action, particularly in relation to the senior at the divisional and district levels. In fact, heavy desk work left them with a little time for the actual extension work. Moreover, there were certain practical difficulties; (i) due to limited resources, multi-pronged attack was not possible; (ii) No priority list was prepared to solve the immediate problems in the rural areas.[10]

A committee appointed under the chairmanship of Sh. Balwant Rai Mehta suggested some measures for the effective execution and implementation of the Community Development projects. The committee[11] stressed the need of involving people in the various schemes of the programme. The committee deplored the lack of representative and democratic institutions to supply the local interest, supervision and care necessary to ensure that expenditure of money upon local projects confirms with the needs and wishes of the locality. He recommended three-tier system for devolution of power and a decentralisation of machinery by popular representative of the local area. In the Punjab, this process was stimulated in the Third Plan by introducing *Panchayati Raj* which was formally inaugurated on 2nd October, 1961. The primary object of this *Raj* was to enable the people of each area to acnieve intensive and continuous development in the interest of entire population. This programme led to the reorganisation of the *Panchayat* as an elected body at the village level and the creation of new institutions at the block and district levels. These new institutions at the block and district levels were known as *Gram Panchayat, Panchayat Samiti* and *Zila Parishad*, respectively. These institutions represented a distinct level of responsibility and functioned with the general schemes of administration. They were responsible for mobilising extensive popular participation in the community development programme at the village, block and district levels.

Panchayati Raj was considered to be the remedy of removing all possible ills of the rural society. But this fact has not been established after the establishment of these institutions. In fact *Panchayati Raj* system is being more and more politicised. It is also noticed that there was a contrast between a promising start and vicissitudes. The main pitfalls of this programme have been the postponement of the elections of these organisations for a long period, frequent suppressions, suspension of *Zila Parishads* and other tiers of *Panchayati Raj*.[12]

After the Community Development Programme several

programmes of development in the rural areas have been undertaken. These include Intensive Agricultural Development Programme, HYVs Programme, Small Farmers Development Agency, Marginal Farmers and Agricultural Labourers Agency and Integrated Rural Development Programme.

Approaching Towards Green Revolution

Intensive Agricultural Development Programmes (IADP)

The Government decided to restructure the Community Development Programme (CDP) and put more emphasis on increasing agricultural production. It was thought that CDP was not suitable for the rapid modernisation of agriculture. The Government of India appointed an Indo-American team in 1959 to inquire into the causes of persistent food shortages and steps to meet it.[13] In the same year U.N. Mission expressed the views that 'in view of the over shadowing danger of starvation the CDP must put priority on increasing agricultural production'.[14] In 1960, the Intensive Agricultural District Programme (IADP) was selectively introduced throughout the country. The IADP marked a distinctive shift in emphasis from a community approach of development to agricultural development. The deepening food crisis in India made it necessary to lay greater stress on agricultural production. The community development approach was not formally abandoned. It still figures in the State budget proposals. But the popular attitude to it has become distinctly lukewarm.

Indo-American team (1959) suggested that the surest way to achieve significant yield break through with rapid increase in over-all production was to concentrate efforts in the 'most responsive areas', where the infusion of science and technology would yield the maximum benefits. The irrigated areas could easily absorb the new technologies. Therefore, in 1961, the IADP approach emphasised the use of a package of improved practices viz. minor irrigation works, introduction of improved seeds, fertilisers, plant protection measures etc. This programme was popularly known as 'Package Programme'.

The IADP was initiated in the selective districts of the country. The selection of the district was based on the following factors:

(a) having maximum assured supply of water;
(b) a minimum of natural hazards;

(c) relatively well-developed village institutions such as co-operative and *Panchayat* and

(d) maximum potential for increasing output within a comparatively short time.

In the first instance seven districts were selected, four from rice region, two from wheat region and one from millet region. In the Punjab State, Ludhiana district was selected under IADP. Later on this programme was extended to other districts too. Among the 15 districts selected in the first and second attempts of the programme in India, the average size of the farm was the largest in Ludhiana, i.e., 7.5 hectares. Ludhiana was also found to be the best among the various districts for infrastructure needed for agricultural development. IADP put more emphasis on strengthening the institutional base, and particularly on building up to a strong financial structure of the co-operative. These efforts were made for timely and adequate supplies of modern inputs to farmers within their reach.

The administrative set-up of the IADP district was as under. The entire work at the district level was controlled by the Deputy Commissioner. He was assisted by one Pilot Project Officer — a senior technocrat of the Department of Agriculture. He was provided with six subject-matter specialists, one each in Agronomy, Soil Science, Horticulture, Plant Protection, Farm Management and Animal Husbandry at district level. These specialists of their departments guided the junior staff and farmers. Pilot Project Officer was also assisted by one Deputy Registrar of Co-operative Societies. Deputy Registrar of Co-operatives was responsible for making assessment of the requirements and making suitable arrangements for the timely and sufficient supplies of crucial inputs viz. improved seeds, fertilisers, pesticides and credit to the farming community.

At block level and village level, the set-up was very much like CDP. But the number of Extension Officers, both Agricultural and Co-operative, and VLWs in each block were increased to effectively implement the package programme and individual farm plan. The number of Agricultural Extension Officers (AEOs) was expanded to five, where as that of VLWs to twenty per IADP block.

The recruitment and placement of this additional staff was itself a difficult task. The procedures for financial clearances and recruitment did not help in many ways. Some of the standard rituals viz. formal approval of the Government of India, sanction by the State government, recruitment machinery, screening of the candidates etc., for the appointment of the staff consumed considerable amount of time and money. Therefore, when IADP was extended to Ferozepur and Sangrur districts in 1971, the departmental staff was diluted substantially to economise on funds. New IADP districts had only 10 VLWs and 3 AEOs at the grass-roots. The Pilot Project Officer was provided with only three subject-matter specialists. Any how, it was experienced that this economy in the budgetary provision was reflected in a relatively poor performance of advisory service in the new IADP districts.[15]

There were significant differences between IADP and generalised CDP. IADP was a sectoral development programme concerned only with agriculture, whereas CDP was a general development programme. In IADP all those farmers having prepared the production plan according to the programme were expected to be given credit facilities. But in case of CDP, the credit disbursement was based on credit worthiness of the person.

The IADP was a pioneer programme for the development of a vital sector of rural development. As a result of the measures taken in the programme and efforts of the peasantry the total wheat production increased from 17.25 lakh tonnes in 1960-61 to 23.60 lakh tonnes in 1964-65 and that of rice production rose from 2.36 lakh tonnes to 3.51 lakh tonnes during the same period in the Punjab. This increase in production was mainly due to extension of area under cultivation and not due to the increase in productivity. The State had 5.5 per cent annual growth rate of agricultural produce against the population growth rate of 3.1 per cent during 1961-66.

There were some criticisms levelled against this programme in the Punjab. IADP favoured the concentration of resources in a limited area and discriminated against the other parts of the State. It made the rich farmers richer and poor one poorer. It might be because of the fact that the rich farmers were quick to adopt the new technology and were able to buy the inputs and machinery. The IADP districts were over-staffed and the scarce administrative resources were over concentrated there.

New Agricultural Strategy or HYV Programme

In 1965-66, another intensive agriculture programme of High Yielding Varieties (HYV) was introduced, which again followed the strategy of introduction in areas with minor changes in the number of officials working under IADP programme. In 1966, the high yielding semi-dwarf wheat varieties of Mexican origin were introduced in the State. A few years after the introduction of this programme, it brought a wheat revolution. In the subsequent years HYVs of rice and other crops were also adopted by the farmers of the State. The new seed — fertiliser — irrigation technology contributed significantly to the recent increase in agricultural productivity and production.

The area under HYVs in the Punjab had been increasing since IADP. Now almost whole of the rice and wheat area is under new seeds. Similarly over 40 per cent of maize area and 80 per cent of cotton area are under HYVs. It has been found that the spread of the area under HYVs was more rapid in areas covered by IADP owing to a well institutional base, availability of package of inputs and a vigorous State government action.

In general, the percentage of farmers adopting HYVs and fertilisers use increased with the increase in the farm size. Table 2.1 shows per acre use of seeds and fertilisers by farm size group in Punjab in 1974-75. There was a positive relationship between farm size and the use of other inputs. It is evident that small farmers lagged behind the large farmers in the adoption of this programme. This gap in adoption was due to some non-neutral factors such as credit, extension services etc. rather than due to the characteristics of new agricultural strategy.

New agricultural technology increased the production and productivity of the agriculture in Punjab. The production of wheat was merely 1916 thousand tonnes in 1965-66 which increased to 5145 thousand tonnes in 1970-71 and 11576 thousand tonnes in 1988-89. Similarly the production of rice increased from 293 thousand tonnes in 1965-66 to 688 thousand tonnes in 1970-71 and 5442 thousand tonnes in 1987-88.

The Punjab has become the food basket of India. It contributes about 56 per cent of wheat and 78 per cent of rice to the Central Pool every year. However, there were two major limitations of the programme: (i) the programme, by and large, benefited already better-off farmers. The gains of the programme could not percolate down to the rural poor of the society. A number of studies[16] concluded that the extent of income disparity had risen because of the introduction of high yielding varieties programme; (ii) it bypassed those regions of the State which were not endowed with assured irrigation or adequate rain fall. In other words it is evident that the new agricultural technology has brought in a certain degree of prosperity to the country side. Relatively larger and well-placed cultivators in the Punjab have been in a position to take full advantage of this economic progress due to their better accessibility to essential requisite for agricultural development. But the economic position of small land holders and landless could not improve proportionately. Therefore, the need for target group approach was felt.

TABLE 2.1: Per acre use of Seeds and Fertilisers by Farm size Group; Punjab in 1974-75

(Rs.)

Farm Size (acres)	Per acre Expenditure in 1974-75 on	
	Seeds	Manure and Fertilizers
Below 2.5	35.31	92.82
2.0-4.99	33.03	97.95
5.0-7.49	35.14	98.19
7.5-12.49	35.15	100.02
12.5-24.99	35.45	112.46
25.0 +	38.27	112.26
Overall	35.51	105.24

Source: Adopted from Bhalla and Chadha, *Green Revolution and the Small Peasants: A Study of Income Distribution among Punjab Cultivators*, New Delhi, Concept Publishing Co., 1983.

Target Group Approach and Village Development Programme

From the above discussion, it is evident that HYVs programme, which was launched on a large-scale from Kharif 1966 in Punjab, increased the production and productivity of agriculture tremendously. The Punjab became the pioneer State of Indian Union for the successful implementation of new agricultural technology. This was obviously a result of combined efforts of planners, scientists, extension workers and the farmers. But the gains of this new technology was not equally shared by the various sections of rural society. The gains mostly went to the well-to-do farmers, who not only had easy access to technology but also to credit. As a result economic inequalities in rural areas of the Punjab were accentuated by way of large farmers becoming richer and the small farmers not getting their share of the benefits of green revolution.

In 1969, the All India Rural Credit Review Committee set-up by the Reserve Bank of India submitted its report. The committee studied the available data and suggested some specific measures to uplift the weaker sections of the rural society, particularly farming society. The committee noted, "it is all the more necessary that the less affluent cultivators should be enabled, through State and institutional support, to improve their production potential and levels of income by adopting improved agricultural practices. If the fruit of development continued to be denied to a large section of the rural community, while prosperity accrues to some, the resulting tensions, social and economic, may not only upset the process of orderly and peaceful change in the rural economy but even frustrate the national efforts to step up agricultural production".[17]

Small Farmers Development Agency (SFDA) and Marginal Farmers and Agricultural Labourers Agency (MFALA)

On the basis of the recommendation of the committee two agencies, SFDA and MFALA, were established. With the help of these agencies, the focus of rural development programmes shifted from mere growth to growth with social justice. The programmes of these agencies were confined to the target groups to adopt new agricultural technology and diversify their farm economy through subsidiary activities such as animal husbandry, dairing, poultry, horticulture etc.

These programmes have been in operation since 1971 and covered 76 blocks in the Punjab. These programmes were merged in Integrated Rural Development Programme (IRDP) in the year 1980. Up to 1978, five projects were working under SFDA in the Punjab. The programmes had some weaknesses also. The identification of the target group posed a big problem because of the paucity of authentic land records. As a result, the persons identified for assistance formed only a segment of the target group. Even the identified persons were not adequately helped due to lack of credit flows. The lower coverage and partial success was mainly due to the stark inadequacies of the main implementing agencies and lack of co-ordination among concerned Government Departments. The various programmes initiated under these agencies did not result in any specific additional asset creation, though the programmes did create some employment opportunities.

Despite the weaknesses of the programmes, they drew the attention of the planners and policy-makers towards the most vulnerable section of the rural society. Greater attention was given to the concept of small and marginal farmers who were largely based on agricultural avocation. It was found necessary to supplement the income of the weaker section through subsidiary occupation viz., animal husbandry, fishery, piggery, poultry and in some cases cottage industry too. This led to the conjoint rise in non-farm activities with regular farm activities. The concept of agriculture itself gradually widened. This had led to a concerted full utilisation of the available income possibilities to a rural family. The seeds of the concept of 'integration' are noticeable in these programmes.[18]

Model Village Scheme

The Model Village Scheme was started in the Punjab during the year 1969-70. This scheme was launched to provide better amenities of life to the rural people. In the first phase of this scheme, certain civic amenities were to be provided through the pavement of streets, construction of drains and disposal of sullage water etc. To begin with 973 villages were taken up under this scheme. It was proposed to spend one lakh rupees on each village which meant an expenditure of Rs. 9.73 crores. About 30 per cent of the villages so selected were big enough to complete the above mentioned works within the specified amount of Rs. one lakh while the pavement of streets and construction of drains in most of the other villages remained incomplete and sanitation remained unsatisfactory. Moreover, this scheme only aimed at the improvement of environmental conditions in the village. It had no linkage to any economic programme.

Jayanti Village Scheme

The Jayanti Village Scheme was launched for development of 117 villages, one per block to mark the 25th anniversary of Independence. The scheme aimed at merely the improvement of environmental conditions and construction of infrastructure in the selected villages and provision of amenities such as paved streets and *pucca* drains etc. A sum of Rs. 50,000 was proposed to spend in each village on these activities. This amount was provided on an *ad hoc* basis and it was insufficient to complete the works contemplated under the scheme. Like model village scheme, this scheme also met with little success. It was not supported by any economic programme.

Food for Work Programme

This programme was launched in 1977 as a non-plan scheme to augment the funds of the State Government for the maintenance of public works on which large investment had been made in the past. The programme did not make much headway in the beginning due to certain constraints inherent in the scheme itself. On review of its progress and the difficulties experienced by the State Government, the scheme has been liberalised to include all on-going plan and non-plan works and new items of public and community works. The basic objectives of the programme were to generate additional employment in rural areas in the lean agricultural seasons and create durable community assets which would strengthen the rural infrastructure. The workers were paid in foodgrains for the job done by them.

The programme showed good results for the first three years of its inception. But, in view of the short-comings and/or need for revamping the programme, it was recasted in July 1980 as the National Rural Employment Programme (NREP), and made an integral part of the Sixth Plan. NREP is explained in this chapter later on.

The basic objectives[19] of the Food for Work Programme were as follows:

(i) To generate additional gainful employment to large number of unemployed and the under-employed persons both men and women, in the rural areas which will improve their incomes and consequently their nutritional level,

(ii) To create durable community assets and strengthen the rural infrastructure, which will result in higher production and better living standard in the rural areas, and

(iii) Utilisation of surplus foodgrains for development of human resources.

For the selection of the beneficiaries, 75 per cent weightage was accorded to the population of agricultural labourers and marginal farmers and 25 per cent weightage to the incidence of poverty.

In the first-year of the programme (1977-78), the employment generation was negligible, i.e., only 0.14 lakh mandays only. But in the subsequent years the programme showed a good success. The total employment generated during 1978-79 was 49.93 lakh mandays. In India, 1979-80 was the year of severe drought, therefore, this programme helped a lot to the poor people. But the impact of the drought in the Punjab was almost negligible. Therefore, the employment generation in 1979-80 decreased from the previous year to only 32.28 lakh mandays. As stated earlier, the programme was converted into NREP in 1980. Up to September 1980, 1.09 lakh mandays of employment were generated under Food For Work Programme.

The programme helped in stabilising the prices of foodgrains in rural areas. It ensured the payment of minimum wages to rural labourers. It also generated additional employment for rural poor.

However, the programme suffered from several limitations in respect of planning and supervision of works. Its operation on a year-to-year basis had resulted in uncertainty about its continuance for the full plan period. The State Government was least interested in building the required technical and administrative support to effectively plan, monitor and over-see the programme. It is found that works of low priority and dubious utility were undertaken under the programme. Most of the time work was executed by the contractors due to lack of administrative and technical support.

The above discussion clearly shows that the programmes such as IADP and HYVs programme etc., were meant for increasing agricultural production in rural areas. These programmes were aimed at intensified development of a particular sector, i.e., agriculture of the rural economy only. These programmes increased the agricultural production substantially. But the gains of these programmes were confined to already prosperous regions and affluent farmers of the State. It became necessary to reassess the impact of the agricultural prosperity. In 1970 Centrally-sponsored schemes for small farmers and marginal farmers and agricultural labourers were started in a few districts and subsequently extended to the rest of the districts by the State Government. These schemes were meant for the weaker sections of the rural society and remained isolated from the general developmental activities in the rural areas in the Punjab. Model village scheme and Jayanti Village Scheme were initiated for the improvement of environmental conditions and they were also not linked to any development activity.

Integrated Rural Development Programmes

We have made it clear that the most of the programmes started before

1970 emphasised on the growth of Gross Domestic Product (GDP)/State Domestic Product (SDP) and 'trickle down' of benefits to the poor. The contribution towards growth was limited to a few people and rural areas. The poor trickle down of the benefits of development increased the economic inequalities among the various groups in rural areas of the economy.

The change in the programmes of development had been noticed after the year 1970. In the new programmes the stress was laid on direct attack on poverty and allowed the GDP to take care of itself instead of focusing on GDP to take care of poverty. While the programmes such as SFDA and MFALA and Minimum Needs Programmes were limited in coverage and confined to a section of target groups, the Integrated Rural Development Programme was having wide coverage, inclusive of all the on going programmes of rural development. IRDP contains the programmes such as SFDA and MFALA. Other programmes such as National Rural Employment Programme (NREP) and RLEGP are directed towards combating the curse of rural poverty through wage employment. In these models of rural development while the growth continues to get its due place, the main thrust is on directly helping the target groups in the rural areas and making them a viable entity.

Among many reasons for the poor trickle on the growth to the rural poor, lack of access to the factors of production and physical and human capital are the main. Therefore, most of the on-going programmes of rural development are directed towards fulfiling the twin objectives of providing access to factors of production and physical and human capital. These measures make available the economic opportunities for the rural poor. The basic policy is to divert the funds from institutional sources so as to provide productive assets to the poor and thereby increasing their income. The programmes such as Integrated Rural Development Programme, Training for Rural Youth for Self-Employment, National Rural Employment Programme and Rural Landless Employment Guarantee Programme are of this nature.

Integrated Rural Development Programme (IRDP)

The Planning Commission in its Draft Sixth Five Year Plan (1978-83) visualised an integrated plan of development at the block level, within which a special beneficiary-oriented plan for the poor was to be appropriately fitted. IRDP was started in 1978-79, initially with 2300 blocks in the country. The programme was extended to all the 5011 blocks in the country from 2nd October, 1980. The specific area development programmes such as SFDA, MFALA etc., were merged into IRDP. The programme emphasised the family rather than individual approach in the identification of the beneficiaries.

IRDP in Punjab was initiated in 1978-79 covering only 11 blocks under the control of Development Department. At that time SFDA and MFALA were also operating under the control of Agriculture Department of the state. From 2nd October, 1980, all these programmes were merged into the new IRD Programme under the control of Development Department and it was extended to all blocks in the State. The programme is financed by the Central and State Government on 50 : 50 basis.

IRDP has been conceived essentially as an anti-poverty programme. The main objective of the IRDP is to provide assistance to families living below poverty line to enable them to improve their income and generate employment. The main emphasis of the implementation of this programme in the Punjab is coverage of identified poor rural families (Yellow Card Holders) having annual income below Rs. 3,600 per family unit. A survey to identify weaker sections in Punjab was conducted in 1980. It was found that 7.44 lakh households having annual income of Rs. 3,600 and below per household were identified in rural areas. These identified families were issued yellow cards by the State Government. These families were considered as target population for the purpose of IRDP assistance. It may be mentioned here that the cut-off line for identification of poor families has been raised to Rs. 4,800 since 1985. The target families consist of small farmers, marginal farmers, agricultural labourers, rural artisans and others whose annual family income is below the cut-off point.

The programme envisages grant of subsidies which amount to 25 per cent of the capital cost for small farmers, 33.33 per cent for marginal farmers, agricultural labourers and rural artisans and 50 per cent for tribal beneficiaries. To meet the balance of cost of an asset, credit is provided by the banking institution.

The over all incharge of IRDP in the Punjab at the State level is the Secretary, Rural Development and *Panchayats*. Joint Development Commissioner (IRD) assisted by Deputy Director (Dev.) is responsible for the implementation and co-ordination of the programme at the State level. At the district level, the IRDP is being implemented through the District Rural Development Agencies (DRDAs). The Additional Deputy Commissioner (Dev.) is the Chief Executive Officer. He is responsible for the implementation of the programme at the district level. The ADC (Dev.) is assisted by Assistant Project Officer (APOs) and other supporting staff both technical and non-technical at the headquarters.[20]

During the Sixth Plan, the total credit of Rs. 11,118 lakh was disbursed under IRDP to the beneficiaries for purchasing productive assets. This amount included Rs. 3,715 lakh of subsidies also. During the same time 3.92 lakh beneficiaries were helped. A critical appraisal of the programme is given in the next chapter. Any how, the evaluation studies have mentioned the following major short-comings of the programme.

Almost all the evaluation studies conducted in the State and elsewhere pointed towards the mis-classification of target families. Non-involvement of people's institutions and banks in the survey of identification of target group and selection of beneficiaries was also noticed.

The selection of beneficiaries was not based on *Antyodya* Principle. At the same time the selection of the beneficiaries was also not placed before the *gram sabha* as mentioned in the guidelines of the programme. As a result some of the deserving poor people could not get benefit of this programme. The selection of schemes under the programme had shown that there was a overwhelming bias towards animal husbandry schemes, more particularly milch cattle. While this activity had considerable employment and income potential, it had resulted into shortage of good quality animal, rise in the prices of animals and lack of supporting inputs viz., feed, health cover, marketing etc.

There was delay in the sanction and disbursement of loans by the DRDA and bank. This was mainly due to procedural difficulties and lack of staff at the block/district level and bank level. Therefore, the middle men and officials indulged in malpractices.

The financial allocation and physical targets under the programme were determined on a uniform basis per block, irrespective of the level of development, number of poor people below the poverty line, physical area of district etc. Therefore, the existing inequalities might remain the same.

In the Punjab the block and district plans were not prepared strictly according to the guidelines. This way a very important task of the programme remained unfulfiled.

The most attractive part of the programme was subsidy which a beneficiary received. The local resources were also not used properly while sanctioning the various development schemes.

A lesser proportion of total beneficiaries than the assisted under the programme could cross the poverty line. The recovery of the loans of the programme was also very poor.

A few other studies have showed the merits of the programme. The programme helped in increasing the income and employment of the beneficiaries. The details of the same are discussed in the next chapter.

Thus, we find that there is wide disagreement among different experts regarding the impact of the programme. Despite the short-comings of the programme, it has mobilised the government machinery for helping the poor. It has given some relief to the poor people also. But the quantum of benefits can be increased by removing the short-comings of the programme.

TRYSEM and Rural Employment

Training for Rural Youth for Self-Employment (TRYSEM) aims at equipping rural youth in the 18 to 35 age group with necessary skill and technology to enable them to seek self-employment. This scheme was initiated as a National Scheme from 15th August, 1979 in all blocks. This is a Centrally-sponsored programme. It has been proposed to train at least 40 youth per block, i.e., 4720 youth per year during the Sixth Plan in the Punjab. The training courses have a practical bias on the concept of learning-doing. The training is provided in selected trades in such activities that lead to self-employment. The training is being imparted by the existing training institutions such as Gram Sewak Training Centres, Agriculture and other universities, I.T.I. and other existing State and Central Organisations. A very important mode of training is through Local Service Establishments, Industrial Units, Master Craftsmen, artisans and skilled workers.

The share of Centre and State in this scheme is 50 : 50. The programme has been a great success in the Punjab. It helps the rural youth more than its target. The scheme provides for the payment of stipend to trainees, honourarium to the trainers and expenses on tool-kits, raw material etc. On completion of the training, trained persons are given assistance by way of loans/subsidy under IRDP to enable them to set-up their ventures. In 1980-81 about 2001 youths were trained and 891 (45 per cent) were self-employed. In 1983-84, the number of persons trained were over 8 times as compared to 1980-81. About 63 per cent of 16331 persons trained in that year set-up ventures for self-employment. During the Sixth Plan 54095 youths were actually trained which were more than double of the target. Of the 54095 trained youths 30795 youths (57%) were self-employed.

Most of the studies evaluating the TRYSEM have reported that there is lack of confidence among the trainees for self employment ventures. There are certain problems of the trainees to get raw material and marketing of the product produced. There is a view that it would be difficult for rural youth from poor families to set-up self-employment ventures and it will be better for them to go in for wage-employment.[21]

National Rural Employment Programme (NREP)

Rural unemployment and under-employment which particularly effect the poorest segments of the rural population have been the major contributory factors to the high incidence of poverty in the rural areas notwithstanding the economic development during the past four decades. In the rural economy a sizeable number of rural population become redundant particularly in the agriculturally lean seasons. Growing poverty as well as malnutrition are the results of this situation. The Sixth Five Year Plan had alleviation of rural poverty as one of the main objectives, the strategy adopted aimed at redistribution of income and consumption in favour of the poorer sections of the population by significantly increasing employment opportunities in the rural areas. The National Rural Employment Programme was started in October 1980 to achieve this objective.

The NREP replaced the Food For Work Programme and became a part of the Sixth Five Year Plan from April 1981. It has been designed mainly to provide employment to the needy in the rural areas in the slack agricultural seasons. The importance of employment programmes in reducing rural poverty is reflected in the Approach to the Seventh Five Year Plan (1985-90) which emphasises food, work and productivity; and has the objective of productive employment to every one seeking it and assigning priority to activities which contribute most effectively to this purpose.[22]

The programme has three basic objectives:[23]

(i) Generation of additional gainful employment for the unemployed and under-employed persons, both men and women in rural areas;

(ii) Creation of durable assets for strengthening rural infrastructure which lead to rapid growth of rural economy and steady rise in the income levels of the rural poor; and

(iii) Improvement of nutritional status and the living standard of the rural poor.

The programme is being implemented as a centrally-sponsored scheme on 50 : 50 basis between Centre and the State. The centre will provide its share in the form of foodgrains to the extent surplus foodgrains are available and rest in cash. The ratio between material component and wage component in respect of individual work is to be 40 : 60 while the overall limit for material component is not to exceed 33 per cent in any district of the State.

In the Punjab, this programme is mainly being implemented by two departments viz., Rural Development and Panchayats and the Forest Department. During the year 1983-84, an amount of Rs. 550 lakh (including 50 per cent central share of Rs. 275 lakhs) was provided under this Scheme. Out of the total outlay, Rs. 55 lakhs were kept for 'Social Forestry' at the disposal of Forest Department and Rs. 495 lakhs for pavement of 'Streets and Construction of Drains', placed at the disposal of R.D. Department. In the same year, the employment of 17.45 lakh mandays was generated. The outlays and physical achievements of the programme are shown in Table 2.2. Similarly in 1984-85, a total sum of Rs. 630.26 lakh was spent and it generated 17.06 lakh mandays of employment.

This programme is continued in Seventh Plan also. In 1985-86, an amount of Rs.757.73 lakhs was spent. With this amount an additional employment of 27.34 lakh mandays was generated. Under NREP, an amount of Rs. 506 lakhs was spent in 1987-88 and generated employment of 17.65 lakh mandays.

It is proposed to spend Rs. 532 lakhs on the various works in 1988-89 and these works are expected to generate employment of 13.38 lakh mandays.

The creation of durable assets was an important objective of this programme and, in fact, this was the real difference betwen the food for work programme and the NREP. In the Punjab, mainly two types of assets are created under NREP, such as social frestry and pavement of streets and construction of drains. The Forest Department does plantation work on community/*Panchayats*' lands to create durable assets. In 1984-85, the Forest Department did plantation work in 1600 hectares of land. It is proposed to complete the plantation work in 2000 hectares in the year 1988-89 against the likely average of 1810 hectares during 1987-88. Out of 12188 villages in the Punjab, 7310 villages have been adopted for pavement work up to 30th June 1987 with the assistance from State Government. Out of these villages, only 752 villages have been covered in their entirety.

TABLE 2.2: The expenditure Incurred and Employment Generated under NREP in Punjab

Item/Year	Sixth Plan						
	1983-84	1984-85	1980-85	1985-86	1986-87	1987-88	1988-89*
Farm Forestry (Lakh Rs.)	55.00	61.46	716.0	157.61	91.20	126.50	133.00
Pavement of Streets & Construction of drains (Lakh Rs.)	518.30	568.80	1754.0	600.73	337.00	379.50	399.00
Total Expenditure (Central + State)	573.30	630.26	2480.0	757.73	428.20	506.00	532.00
Employment Generated (Lakh Mandays)	17.45	17.06	103.0	27.34	19.04	17.65	13.38

* Proposed.

Source: Compiled from Annual Plan, 1988-89 and Annual Administration Report of Rural Development & Panchayats Department, Punjab of different years.

The foregoing analysis clearly shows that the gainful employment generation target under the NREP is consistently achieved. However, there are certain drawbacks which are generally reported against this programme. First, it is not known that who are the actual beneficiaries of NREP, i.e., how many of them are landless and poorest among the poor. It is felt that NREP lacks a direct attention on the target groups for whom the programme is intended. The selection of beneficiaries under this programme is not proper. Secondly, as per the guidelines of NREP, a proportion of the funds has been ear-marked for works of direct benefit to members of scheduled castes who were among the poorest of the poor.[24] Such works include drinking water wells, minor irrigation wells, construction of link roads, construction of *harijan chaupals* and sanitation work. Despite the increase in expenditure, it is not clear whether the ear-marked funds are spent for the pruposes mentioned above. Moreover, sufficient details of the types of works taken up in this category are not available with us. Moreover, the quality of the assets is also poor.

Thirdly, the wage rate paid under the programme is considered to be very low and hence the scheme is not attractive to the wage earning class. Further, delay in payment of wages has also been reported by some of the studies.

The works implemented through NREP are not co-ordinated and integrated with the requirements of the families identified for assistance under IRDP. The works are not being decided as is expected through popular participation and consultation with *Panchayat* and *Gram Sabha*.

It is also felt that the programme has not been able to make any dent on seasonal unemployment and under-employment. Since NREP continues to remain a major feature of the Seventh Plan, therefore, to make judicious use of funds spent on it, it is necessary to review and redesign the programme to make it more effective in ameliorating mass poverty from rural areas through gainful employment.

Rural Landless Employment Guarantee Programme (RLEGP)

Like NREP this programme also generates gainful wage employment for a large section of rural poor, i.e., landless labourers. It has, however, been felt for some time that hardcore of rural poverty particularly pertaining to employment opportunities for the landless workers during the lean agricultural periods, when work is scarce, has to be tackled in a more direct and specific manner. Accordingly, a new scheme called 'Rural Landless Employment Guarantee Programme', has been commenced with effect from 15th August, 1983.

This scheme was initiated in the State during 1983-84 as a 100 per cent centrally-sponsored scheme with the following objectives:

(i) to improve and expand employment opportunities particularly for the rural landless labour with a view to providing guarantee of employment to atleast one member of every rural landless household up to 100 days in a year.

(ii) to create productive and durable assets for direct and continued benefits to the poverty groups and for strengthening rural economic and social infrastructure which will lead to rapid growth of rural economy and steady rise in the employment opportunities and income level of the rural poor;

(iii) to improve the overall quality of life in the rural area.

This programme is implemented in Punjab by District Rural Development Agency. In order to achieve the basic objectives of providing employment through creation of durable productive assets, at least 50 per cent of the funds for a project as a whole are to be utilised as wage component. Any how in the guidelines[25] it has been made clear that it is open to the State Government to exceed the ceiling of non-wage component provided the extra cost on this account is met by the State Government out of the funds other than those provided under this programme.

The assistance under this programme is being provided by Government of India on the basis of following criterion:

(a) 50 per cent weightage is given to the number of agricultural labourers and marginal farmers in the State;

(b) 50 per cent weightage is given to the incidence of poverty in the State.

It is clear from the above discussion that RLEGP seeks to provide gainful employment to landless -- gainful to the individual as well as to the community. There are, thus, twin objectives of the programme, namely (i) employment generation and (ii) formation of productive assets. By the end of Sixth Five Year Plan, the total central assistance made available to the State amounted to Rs. 6.75 crores for various projects, viz., construction of 110 Mahila Mandal Bhawans, plantation of 123.70 lakh plants, 451 village ponds for fish culture and 45 fish nurseries, pavement of streets and construction of drains in 46 villages under 'Environment Improvement' and construction of 500 primary school buildings to generate employment of 20.95 lakh mandays.

Table 2.3 shows that during 1985-86 and 1986-87 the funds utilised under the programme were Rs. 671 and Rs. 968 lakhs respectively. During 1985-86, 20.69 lakh mandays of employment were generated against the target of 17.54 lakh mandays of employment. In the same year other achievements of the programme were plantation of 70.40 lakh plants, 377 fish ponds, repair of 209 schools and construction of 1500 houses under *Indira Awass Yojna.* In 1985-86, the wheat is proposed to be available to the workers engaged under RLEGP at the subsidised rate of Rs. 1.50 per kg.[27] During 1986-87, 18.02 lakh mandays of employment was generated against the target of 15 lakh mandays. The physical achievement of the programme was the plantation of 37.83 lakh plants on 1890 hectares, 172 fish ponds, construction of 2583 houses, reclamation of 3350 acres of *Kallar* land and construction of 1218 latrines and 11 community centres.

TABLE 2.3: Funds Utilisation and Physical Achievements of RLEGP

(Rs. in Lakhs)

Assets	1983-85		1985-86		1986-87	
	A	B	A	B	A	B
(i) Development of Rural Arboriculture including Social Forestry/Nurseries	—	123.70 lakh plants 8400 ha	166.50	70.40 lakh plants 4024 ha	94.00	37.83 lakh plants 1890 ha
(ii) Development of Fish Ponds/Nurseries	—	45 Fish Nurse-ries	163.01	377 Fish Ponds	76.13	172 Fish Ponds
(iii) Construction of Primary School Buildings	—	500 Schools	87.61 16.72 100.00	209 Schools	90.72 294.03	191 Sc-hools**
(iv) Rural Houses for S.Cs.	—	—	137.00	1500 Houses	227.29	2583 Houses
(v) Anti-Water Logging Work	—	—	—	—	100.56	88 Works
(vi) Reclamation of *Kallar/ Banjar* Lands	—	—	—	—	63.42	3350 acres
(vii) Construction of Rural Latrines/Pavement of Streets & Drains	—	46 Village pave-ments	—	—	11.40	1218 Latrines
(viii) Construction of multi-purpose Community Centres	—	110 Mehila Mandals	—	—	10.48	11 Centres
Total:	675.00		670.84		968.03	
Employment Generated (Lakh Mandays)		20.95		20.69		18.02

** 1985-86; A = Funds Utilised and B = Physical Achievements

Source: As in Table 2.2

RLEGP provides wage employment to a specific category of rural people who are largely below the poverty line. This programme is important for employment generation and anti-poverty programme as well as rural development in general. The programme ensures the employment to atleast one member of the household of a landless beneficiary. The weaknesses of this programme are similar to NREP. Any how, some more shortcomings of the programme are given below:

In the programme guidelines, it is envisaged that 50 per cent of the total cost of the project would be spent on wages. It is not mentioned what weightage should be given to skilled and unskilled labourers. In the rural areas there are both skilled and unskilled wage earners. But, most of the landless labourers are unskilled. If most of the skilled labourers are employed for completing the projects then a major part of the wages will be spent on them. Therefore, a major part of landless labourers, i.e., unskilled labourers will not benefit from this programme.

The programme emphasises that only productive and labour intensive projects should be undertaken. The planning and formation of these projects may be a very difficult task. It is mainly because of the fact that it is difficult to define and quantify productivity of the projects. For example, in the Punjab much of the funds have been utilised for social forestry, village fish ponds, schools, houses for SCs and construction of rural latrines/drains and pavement of streets. Almost all these projects indirectly generate benefits. Therefore, it is difficult to assess the impact of the projects adopted under the programme on the increase in productivity.

The RLEGP will have only short-term wage employment benefits. In other words the landless labourer will get benefit from the project so long it is continuing. But the assets generated by this employment are permanent and improve the economic welfare of the people. It is doubtful that the benefit of these projects would become available to the rural poor.

NOTES

1. Walter C. Neale, "The Changing Structure of the rural Economy", appeared in, *The Growth of Rural Economy*, (Ed.), Department of Economics, P.U. Chandigarh, 1960.
2. C.N. Ray, "Rural Development Programmes in India", *Man and Development*, 1985.
3. IRDP in Punjab; Project Report for 1977-78 to 1981-82, Government of Punjab, Chandigarh.

4. *Punjab: Socio-Economic Strides in Development (1947-87)*, published by Director of Information and Public Relations, Punjab, p. 17.
5. A.S. Kahlon *et al.*, Organisational and Institutional implications of rapid growth and commercialisation of Punjab Agriculture, PAU, Ludhiana, 1974, p. 4.
6. The data were obtained from Socio-Economic Development Strides, *op cit.*
7. S.C. Dube, "Unrealised utopias and widening disparities", in L.P. Vidyarthi (ed.), *Rural Development in South Asia*, Concept Publishing Co., New Delhi, 1982.
8. Report of the State Evaluation Committee on the Working of the Community Development Programme in the Punjab, Development Department (C.P.) Punjab, Chandigarh, Controller of Printings and Stationers, Punjab, February 15, 1960.
9. Walter C. Neale, *op. cit.*
10. A.S. Kahlon, *op. cit.* p. 12.
11. Report of the Team for the Study of Community Project and National Extension Service, 3 vols, Planning Commission, Delhi, 1957.
12. For example the last election held to *Village Panchayat* in 1983 and of *Panchayat Samitees* and *Zila Parishad* in 1975 in Punjab, whereas the term of these elections is 5 years.
13. The Agricultural Production Team Report on India's Food Crisis and steps to meet it, GOI, Ministry of Food and Agriculture and Minisxtry of CD & Co-operation, New Delhi, April, 1959.
14. Report of a C.D. Evaluation Mission in India, United Nations, New York, 1959 (unpublished)
15. A.S. Kahlon, *et el., op. cit.*
16. (a) H.S. Bal and Gurbachan Singh, 'Pattern of Income Distribution in Rural Areas', *IJAE,* XXV (3), 1970.
    (b) P.K. Bhardhan, 'Inequality in Farm Incomes', *EPW*, Annual No., 1974, p. 301 to 307.
    (c) Joginder Singh, 'Income Distribution in Rural Sector of the Punjab', *Indian Economic Journal*, Vol. 25, No. 2, Oct-Dec. 1977.
    (d) R.K. Mahajan, Impact of Improved Farm Technology on Income, Productivity and Employment, Ph.D.Thesis, (Unpublished), Jammu University, 1980.
    (e) Keith Griffen: *The Political Economy of Agrarian Change*, MacMillan Press Ltd., London, 1974, . 69.
17. I.J. Naidu, 'Technology for Small Farmers', *Yojna*, June 1, 1977, p. 29.
18. S.K. Rau, 'Strategies for Rural Development', *Kurukshetra*, March 1, 1980, p. 20.
19. The guidelines for 'Food For Work Programme', Ministry of Agriculture and Rural Development, Government of India, New Delhi.
20. Annual Administration Report of R.D. and Panchayats Department, Punjab, for the year 1984-85, Govt. of Punjab, Chandigarh, p. 4.
21. L.C. Jain, Grass Without Roots, R.D. under Govt. Auspices, ICSSR's Project, 1984, p. 115.
22. Guidelines, National Rural Employment Programme, Govt. of India, Department of Rural Development, Ministry of Agriculture and Rural Development, New Delhi, August, 1985.
23. *Ibid.*
24. Guidelines, *op. cit.*, Annexure I.
25. Instructions for implementation of RLEGP, Govt. of India, Department of Rural Development, Ministry of Agriculture and Rural Development, New Delhi, April, 1985.
27. The wage under RLEGP is paid partly in foodgrains and partly in cash. One kilogram of foodgrains per head per day may be given as part of the wages in foodgrains and the balance amount may be paid in cash.

THREE

DIFFERENTIAL RURAL SCENARIO

THE PUNJAB has shown a very fast rate of growth during the past four decades particularly in agriculture. Its performance in agriculture has been so convincing that it is considered to be the foodgrain -- basket of India. It. is veritable true that the green revolution and other programmes of rural development improved the general condition of the rural areas, but they failed to arrest the menace of poverty, unemployment/under-employment and inequalities in income and wealth as fast as the growth in State Domestic Product. Some of the studies relating to income distribution and poverty expressed the growing inequalities[1] and reversal of poverty trends in rural areas particularly after the year 1966-67.[2] These studies exposed the weakness of India's plan strategy for achieving the twin objectives of growth and social justice.

Despite the tremendous agricultural growth in the Punjab, the pace of decline in people below the poverty line has been slow.[3] The economic inequalities amongst the people in the rural areas have increased. Therefore, it is important to study extent of economic inequalities among different people in the rural Punjab.

In this chapter an attempt is made to study the differential impact of the programmes undertaken so far in the Punjab. The study is based on secondary data collected from various sources.

Here, a study of incidence of poverty in the rural Punjab is undertaken. It points to the growing economic inequalities in the economy, too.

Concept of Poverty

The concept of poverty is explained differently by the various experts. The difference has been drawn between 'relative' and 'absolute' terms of poverty. The 'relative' poverty is generally measured in terms of unequal distribution of income in a country or a State which results out of unequal earnings. Unequal earnings are, in turn, due to unequal opportunities, unequal ownership of assets, unequal land holdings and a host of other institutional factors.

Absolute poverty refers to the inadequacy of income to meet the basic necessities of life. For this purpose, poverty should be conceived in terms of minimum human needs which are considered essential and are capable of being measured objectively. The extent of poverty is the proportion of the population living below this minimum needs called the poverty line.

In July 1962, Gadgil Group[4] set-up by the Planning Commission recommended a per capita consumption of Rs. 20 per month at 1960-61 prices, as the bare minimum level of living in India. This norm has the acceptance of the Indian Planning Commission. Subsequently, a number of economists (Minhas,[5] Vaidyanathan,[6] Johri and Pandey) defined the poverty norm as Rs. 20 per person monthly expenditure in the urban areas and Rs. 15 as its assumed equivalent in the rural areas at 1960-61 prices. Bardhan used a still lower figure, i.e., Rs. 18 for the urban poverty line, whereas the rural poverty line remained at Rs. 15.

Most of the studies (including the present one) have used the NSS data for calculating the incidence of poverty. This is done despite a number of limitations of the data, for example, NSS data present the distribution of population by discrete per capita household expenditure classes. 'The poverty line typically will not coincide with a boundary between expenditure classes'.[7] It is mainly because of the fact that some persons in each averaged group would be typical of that group and there may be many 'well fed yet poor', or 'hungry yet rich', in such group averaging.[8] However, the use of NSS data is popular due to the fact that the NSS data remain a very useful source for the study of Indian economic structure.

The consumption data given by NSSO are at current prices. Therefore, in the present analysis the consumption data for rural areas have been adjusted by taking Consumer Price Index Numbers for Agricultural Labourers as deflator.

Estimates of Poverty

First of all we shall discuss the absolute poverty in the Punjab. Most of the estimates of rural poverty in India are made on the basis of consumption data published by National Sample Survey Organisation (NSSO). A few studies[9] have given the estimates of poverty for rural India. Our analysis is based on the data of rural poverty for the Punjab calculated by M.S. Ahluwalia and C.K. Johri and B.K. Jain. Their poverty estimates rest upon the data for consumer expenditure collected and published almost yearly by NSSO. We shall study 12 years data spread over from 1960-61 to 1973-74.[10] The poverty figures for various States for the year 1977-78 are available from the Draft Sixth Five Year Plan (1980-85).

TABLE 3.1: Percentage of Rural Population in Poverty in Punjab (including Haryana)

Years	Ahluwalia's Study		Johri & Jain's study	
	Punjab	India	Punjab	India
1957-58	28.0	53.4	—	—
1958-59	24.2	48.7	—	—
1960-61	18.8	42.0	14.06	38.26
1961-62	22.3	42.3	19.47	37.44
1963-64	29.4	49.1	23.06	39.39
1964-65	26.5	50.4	20.92	46.08
1965-66	26.5	51.1	22.22	48.63
1966-67	29.5	57.4	21.66	56.02
1967-68	33.9	57.9	27.80	55.79
1968-69	24.0	53.5	18.00	50.33
1969-70	—	—	20.70	49.12
1970-71	23.6	49.1	17.10	47.39
1972-73	21.5	—	17.53	47.08
1973-74	23.0	47.1	17.90	47.25
1977-78	17.56	50.32	17.56	50.32

Source: (i) Ahluwalia, *op. cit.*
(ii) Johri and Jain, *op. cit.*
(iii) For 1977-78, see India's Sixth Five Year Plan, 1980-85, p 16.

The estimates of poverty for the rural areas of the Punjab (including Haryana) are given in Table 3.1. The perusal of the table shows that poverty in the Punjab is not so severe as in India as a whole over the different years. The difference in the figures of percentage of rural population below the poverty line may be due to the difference in the poverty norms adopted by these studies. But the pattern of rise and decline in poverty is almost the same. In both these studies the lowest and the highest figures of poverty are found in 1960-61 and 1967-68, respectively. Table 3.1 shows the erratic trend of rural poverty in the different years in the Punjab. The percentage of population below poverty line increased from 1960-61 to 1967-68, but it started descending its peak since 1967-68. The phenomenon of rural poverty can be better understood if we study the changes of incidence in rural poverty with the help of Table 3.2.

TABLE 3.2: Changes in the Incidence of Rural Poverty in Punjab and Haryana, 1956-57 to 1977-78.

Sub period	Gap in Periods Years	Changes in the percentage of population on below poverty line
1956-57 to 1960-61	4	Down from 28 to 19 %
1960-61 to 1965-66	6	Up from 19 to 27 %
1965-66 to 1967-68	3	Up from 27 to 34 %
1967-68 to 1973-74	7	Down from 34 to 23 %
1973-74 to 1977-78	5	Down from 23 to 18 %

Source: Estimates of the poverty percentage except 1977/78 are taken from M.S. Ahluwalia (1978) *op. cit.*, p. 305. For 1977/78 the average of percentage of population below poverty line of Punjab and Haryana has been taken from Draft Sixth Plan (1980-85) p.16.

Table 3.2. shows the changes in incidence of rural poverty in the Punjab and Haryana. There is decrease in incidence of poverty during 1956-57 to 1960-61. This decline may be due to the land reforms[11] and increase in agricultural production. There was an aggravation of rural poverty between 1960-61 to 1967-68. The percentage of people below poverty line increased from 19 per cent to 34 per cent during the same periods of time. In these years the programmes such as IADP, IAAP and HYP were also introduced in the State. But this period was full of fluctuations of agricultural production. For example, keeping the Index of agricultural production as 100 in 1960-61 in the Punjab, the indices of agricultural production decreased from 100 in the years 1961-62 and 1963-64. The agricultural production increased only after 1967-68. Therefore, in the initial years of intensive agricultural development programmes, the incidence of rural poverty increased in the Punjab mainly due to the fluctuations in the output.

The incidence of poverty has been declining since 1967-68. During 1967-68 to 1973-74, the poverty reduced from 34 per cent to 23 per cent. It may be mainly due to the effect of green revolution. During 1965-66 to 1970-71, the annual compound growth rate of agriculture in the net State domestic product at factor cost (at constant prices) was about 8 per cent. But the decline in percentage of rural population below poverty line was smaller than the agricultural growth rate. It may be due to the fact that 'because of the rural poor's small share in the marketed agricultural surplus; rigidities in rural wages, which were increasingly montiesed; and the widespread dependence of the poor on market purchases for consumption needs, he thought that changes in the nominal price of the consumption basket of the poor had a far greater and more immediate impact on their ability to cross the poverty line than on their incomes whether they were producers of these commodities or farm labourers'.[12] For a better understanding of these results, we have calculated the time trend. The figures in Table 3.1 have been divided into two parts, i.e., from 1960-61 to 1965-66 (pre-green revolution period) and from 1966-67 to 1977-78 (post-green revolution period). Linear time trend has been fitted in the data. The results are shown below:

(a) Based on Ahluwalia's Data

$$BPL_1 = 19.48 + 1.55\ TIME_1 \qquad r^2 = 0.3683$$
$$(1.96)$$
$$BPL_2 = 33.51 - 1.11^{*}\ TIME_2 \qquad r^2 = 0.4789$$
$$(3.46)$$

(b) Based on Johri and Jain's Data

$$BPL_1 = 14.65 + 1.76^{NS}\ TIME_1 \qquad r^2 = 0.3900$$
$$(1.75)$$
$$BPL_3 = 24.78 - 1.17^{NS}\ TIME_3 \qquad r^2 = 0.2000$$
$$(1.66)$$

where:

(i) BPL and TIME are the variables of below poverty line and Time respectively;
(ii) Subscripts 1, 2 and 3 represent for the periods 1960-61 to 1965-66, 1966-67 to 1977-78 and 1966-67 to 1973-74, respectively.
(iii) Figures in parentheses are t-ratios. '*' denotes significant at 5 per cent level and NS means not significant.

The results of linear time trend calculated on the basis of Ahluwalia and Johri's data show that in the pre-green revolution period the incidence of rural poverty was on an increase. The regression coefficients of time for the period 1960-61 to 1965-66 were not statistically significant even at 5 per cent of probability level. The increase in rural poverty in the pre-green revolution period may be mainly due to the fluctuation in agricultural production, rise in the consumer price index for agricultural labourers[13] and stagnant real wages.

The general trend for the incidence of poverty declined after the year 1966-67. This is evident from the negative regression coefficients of time in both the equations. The regression coefficient calculated on the basis of Ahluwalia's data was significant at 5 per cent level.

It is also observed that the decline in poverty in the post-green revolution period was less than the increase in agricultural growth. The annual compound growth rate of agriculture in net SDP between 1965-66 and 1970-71 was 8 per cent per annum, where as the decline in poverty during the same period was about 2 per cent only. It is obvious from this analysis that the green revolution has reduced the rural poverty, but there was a thin trickle of agricultural growth.[14] Some of the reasons for the poor trickle are given below:

(i) There was a slow rise in real wages during 1966 to 1970. The time trend of wages of agricultural labourers shows the same inclination. During 1970-74, the wages in the rural areas declined. The regression coefficient of time for wages for all the operations were negative and significant. Since the main source of livelihood of the target families in the rural areas is wage-employment, a poor growth rate in wages would certainly cast its shadow on the poverty trend rates.

(ii) The new agricultural strategy has tremendously increased the agriculture production, but its gains could not percolate down to poor strata of people in the State. Therefore, it is safe to conclude that the spurt of agricultural production during green revolution could not make a significant dent on rural poverty in the Punjab. A few studies have even reported the decline in annual real wage income per agricultural labour household in Punjab (including Haryana). In 1964-65, the wage income was Rs. 992 which decreased to 887 in 1974-75 (constant prices).[15]

(iii) Inmigration of rural labour from the backward districts of

> Bihar, Rajasthan and Eastern Uttar Pradesh has kept the growth of wage income and reduction of poverty low.[16] Above all institutional factors are biased towards rich farmers and rich lobby in the rural sector.

To sum up, we can say that the data of rural poverty show that there was erratic trend between 1958 to 1978 of the incidence of poverty in the rural Punjab. Improved agricultural performance was associated with decline in incidence of poverty. In the pre-green revolution period, incidence of poverty increased sharply mainly due to fluctuation of agricultural output. But after 1966-67, the agricultural production increased tremendously due to green revolution. This increase in agricultural production has reduced the rural poverty which is clear from the negative regression coefficient. The weak coefficients of determination, r^2s, show that it is better to include some more factors besides time.

Above results show that there are different norms for determining poverty line and divergence in the estimates of incidence of poverty. But it is evident that the people below poverty line reached its peak in 1967-68 and declined afterwards. The minimum level of rural poverty in sixties was in 1960-61 i.e. 19 per cent and in seventies in 1977-78, i.e., 18 per cent. It shows that there was no significant decline in poverty during 1956-57 to 1977-78. During these years the Punjab experienced the green revolution. It is generally said that the benefits of green revolution are distributed in favour of large farmers. It is mainly due to the fact that the present institutional set-up is highly biased towards already privileged class. There is evidence of the persistence of inequalities of consumption expenditure and assets among rural households. The economic position of unprivileged people such as landless labourers, rural artisans, petty shopkeepers, marginal and small farmers etc., has remained almost the same or deteriorated. Here we discuss the inequalities in consumption expenditure, assets, landholdings, credit etc., among different groups.

Consumption Expenditure

The results of the consumer expenditure broadly agree with those of income distribution. The main source of consumer expenditure data is the different rounds of the NSSO. The NSS data provide the expenditure figures for all categories of rural households divided into various Monthly Per Capita Expenditure Classes (MPCE). Consumption level indicates the level of living of the population. MPCE also helps in identifying the poverty cut-off point.

Table 3.3 shows the distribution of consumption expenditure among rural households of the Punjab. The perusal of Table 3.3 shows that per capita expenditure of the rural population of the Punjab has increased by about 50 per cent in 1983 as compared with 1964-65. Total per capita expenditure in each of the expenditure class has also improved. It is observed from Table 3.3 that the improvement in non-food items was marginal in 1983. In 1964-65, 32 per cent of the total expenditure was spent on non-food items, such as *Pan*, tobacco and intoxicants, clothing, fuel and light, consumer durables and other non-food items, whereas this proportion increased to 35 per cent in 1983. In the former period the proportion of non-food expenditure in the various expenditure classes was in the range of 15 to 59 per cent, whereas it increased 26 to 50 per cent in the latter period.

TABLE 3.3: Distribution of Consumption Expenditure Among Rural Households of Punjab

PMCE Class (Rs.)	1964-65 Percentage share in			PMCE Class (1964-65 prices) (Rs.)	1983 Percentage share in		
	Consumer Unit	Food Expenditure	Non-food Expenditure		Consumer Unit	Food Expenditure	Non-food Expenditure
8 - 11	2.85	8.41	1.48	8 - 11	0.13	9.42	2.51
11 - 13	2.25	10.25	2.11	11 - 13	0.49	11.12	3.39
13 - 15	3.75	11.05	2.72	13 - 16	1.08	19.83	3.38
15 - 18	7.11	13.39	3.09	16 - 18	3.32	16.21	4.99
18 - 21	6.74	14.86	4.56	18 - 22	6.22	19.26	6.04
21 - 24	8.66	18.08	4.37	22 - 26	8.62	22.44	7.36
24 - 43	42.12	23.50	4.19	26 - 40	32.90	29.12	11.03
43 - 55	12.26	33.89	14.80	40 - 53	20.65	37.47	16.58
55 - 75	9.63	41.88	21.33	53 - 79	17.75	45.56	28.27
Above 75	4.63	44.70	63.62	Above 79	8.84	67.12	63.70
All Groups	100.00	24.49	11.73	All Groups	100.00	34.89	18.57
		(67.62)	(32.38)			(65.26)	(34.74)

Note: (a) The 1983 Per Month Consumption Expenditure Class have been adjusted to 1964-65 prices by using the Consumer Price Index Number for Middle Classes in Punjab and Classes are rounded to the nearest point.

(b) The 1983 figures for food-items have been deflated to the 1964-65 level by using wholesale price index for wheat in Punjab, and for non-food items using the general price index for the middle clases in Punjab.

Source: The NSS 19th Round (July 1964 - June 1965) and *Sarvekshna*, GOI, Vol. IX, No. 4, April 1986.

Table 3.3 also shows adjusted figures of consumption expenditure of 1983 on the basis of 1964-65 prices. This way we can compare the data between the two years. There were 22.70 per cent and 9.79 per cent of the total consumer units in the poor expenditure classes in the year 1964-65 and1983 respectively. This shows the improvement in the standard of living of the very poor people. In 1964-65, food-items claimed 77 to 86 per cent of total expenditure of the poor classes, but the figures for 1983 were 71 to 74 per cent. It is mainly due to the fact that poor people pay more attention to secure the means of survival first.

In the light of above analysis, it can be said that the condition of rural poor has considerably improved in 1983 as compared with 1964-65. The figures in Table 3.3 clearly show that the green revolution has improved the standard of living of almost all the classes. In the recent period, the rural people allocate more portion of the total budget on non-food items than 1964-65.

On the basis of MPCE Classes in the Punjab, the distribution of consumption expenditure among the various strata of the rural population can be calculated. These results throw light on the relative inequality in the consumption of the various decile groups of persons. In Table 3.4 the share of different decile groups in total consumption has been shown for the years 1960-61, 1970-71 and 1983. The perusal of Table 3.4 shows that the various decile groups show unequal distribution of consumption expenditure. There is a difference of consumption expenditure of the bottom and top 30 per cent of population. In all the three periods the concentration of expenditure was in top 30 per cent of total population. There was no significant shift in the shares of consumption of different deciles of population across the years of pre-green revolution (1960-61), green revolution (1970-71) and post-green revolution (1983). Thus, the above analysis shows that between 1960-61 and 1970-71 the share of bottom 30 per cent population was deteriorated but the condition of top 30 per cent improved. The figures in 1983 showed a slight improvement in the condition of top 30 per cent and middle 40 per cent.

Thus, it may be concluded that green revolution in the Punjab improved the condition of almost all the expenditure classes in the rural areas, but the share of bottom 30 per cent of population in consumption expenditure was degenerated in 1970-71 and was improved in 1983. It may be due to the fact that green revolution has accentuated the inequalities of distribution of consumption expenditure towards privileged rural classes. Therefore, the condition of poor people deteriorated in 1970-71. The improvement in consumption of poor classes in 1983 might be due to poverty alleviation programmes started after 1970s.

TABLE 3.4: Percentage Share of Population in Total Consumption

Population Group	Cumulated percentage in total consumption		
	1960-61	1970-71	1983
1st Decline	4.34	3.79	3.98
2nd Decline	10.40	8.94	9.23
3rd Decline	16.83	14.85	15.80
4th Decline	23.44	21.29	22.86
5th Decline	31.40	29.12	30.78
6th Decline	40.58	37.94	40.12
7th Decline	50.14	48.23	50.00
8th Decline	61.78	60.57	61.85
9th Decline	76.84	75.33	76.02
10th Decline	100.00	100.00	100.00
Bottom 30 per cent	16.83	14.85	15.80
Middle 40 per cent	33.31	33.38	34.20
Top 30 per cent	49.86	51.77	50.00

Source: For 1960-61 and 1970-71, See Indira Rajaraman, *op. cit.* The figure for 1983 have been calculated by the author from *Sarvekshna*, Vol. IX, No.4, April 1986, Govt. of India, New Delhi.

Consumption of Electricity

The Minimum Needs Programme (MNP) was introduced in the Fifth Five Year Plan and continued even in the Seventh Plan. This programme is an investment in human resource development by providing free or subsidised services through public agencies to improve the consumption level of those living below the poverty line. Out of a package of eight components for a beneficiary, the rural electrification programme is one of the important components. The Punjab has electrified 100 per cent of its villages in 1976. But there are lot of inequalities in the consumption of electricity for domestic use in rural sector of the Punjab. The data for calculating inequalities in the consumption of electricity has been taken from thirty-first round of NSS (July 1976 - June 1977).[17] The share of domestic consumption of electricity by the households in the electrified villages is calculated and presented in Table 3.5. In the Punjab, the lower 10 per cent and lower 20 per cent of the households in the electrified villages were consuming 8.24 per cent and 16.65 per cent of electricity power respectively for domestic purpose, whereas the upper 10 and 20 per cent households were consuming 12.39 and 24.35 per cent of electric power respectively. The condition of lower poor classes further deteriorated when the analysis was carried on the individual basis in the electrified villages. It is found that lower 10 and 20 per cent persons in the electrified villages in the Punjab were consuming 6.64 and 13.54 per cent of electric power for domestic purposes, whereas the upper 10 and 20 per cent persons in the same villages were consuming 15.63 and 29.66 per cent respectively. The NSS survey reveals that 76 per cent of households in the electrified villages in the Punjab stated reasons for non-use of electricity as 'cannot afford'. Thus it is clear that poor people in the rural areas were not in a position to afford a very important facility, i.e., electricity.

TABLE 3.5: The Share of Domestic Consumption of Electricity of the Households/Population in Electrified Villages in Punjab

(Percentage)

Population Household Group	Share of domestic consumption of electricity	
	Household	Population
Lower 10%	8.24	6.64
Lower 20%	16.65	13.54
Upper 20%	24.35	29.66
Upper 10%	12.39	15.63

Source: *Sarvekshana, op.cit.*

Limited Access to Land

Land is one of the most important asset in rural areas which determines the economic position of the people. It also determines the degree of inequality in rural areas. It is vertible true that the new agricultural strategy benefited more to the big farmers than small farmers who are rightly called laggards of the strategy.

It has been brought forth by a number of studies and surveys conducted for the identification of target group families that poverty is concentrated amongst marginal and small farmers and landless labourers in the rural areas. Unfortunately, these classes constitute majority of the rural population but have meagre assets for the improvement of their income. The various agricultural censuses conducted in the Punjab provide very useful data for discussion over here. Amongst the landed classes marginal and small farmers operated most of the holdings, i.e., 57 per cent holdings in 1970-71, 61 per cent in 1976-77 and 39 per cent in 1980-81 (See Table 3.6)..The operational area with them was only 15, 15 and 14 per cent, respectively. As against this, medium and large farmers (4 hectares or more) accounting for 23, 21 and 33 per cent of total agricultural holdings in 1970-71, 1976-77 and 1980-81 and they operated 65, 64 and 67 per cent of the land in the same agricultural census years, respectively. Table 3.6 shows that there is a significant fall in the agricultural holdings in the year 1980-81 as compared with the years 1970-71 and 1976-77. It shows the de-peasantisation in the Punjab Economy.

Despite several laws enacted for land reforms, the concentration of land remained with the medium and large farmers. In order to examine whether the concentration ratio among various classes has significantly changed overtime; the interclass concentration ratio (ICR) has been calculated on the basis of methodology used by Prof. C.T. Kurien.[18] To study ICR he has attempted a comparison of the relative position of the size-group in the two periods.

$$ICR_i = \frac{q_i/Q}{p_i/P} \times 100$$

where, Q is the total area and P is the total number of households; q_i is the area owned and p_i is the number of household in the ith class. The figures for 1970-71 and 1976-77 and 1970-71 and 1980-81 are presented in Table 3.6.

The figures for 1970-71 and 1976-77 show that ICRs of all size classes except the lowest one have gone up. A Chi-square test has been applied to test the significance of the change in the ICR_i's over the two periods. The tabulated value of Chi-square at one degree of freedom is 3.841. On the basis of tabulated value, it is observed that the changes in the ICR_i's of all the groups except the top one are not significant. The changes in the last group of the highest size of holdings is significant and striking. In order to test the significance of the change in the two distribution a weighted[19] Chi-square value is used. The calculated value of weighted Chi-square is found less than the tabulated value of Chi-square which determines that the change has not been significant.

TABLE 3.6: Distribution of Operational Holdings as per Agricultural Censuses

Size Class of Holdings (Hectare)	Percentage of Holdings			Percentage of Area Operated			Inter Class Concentration			Weights		Chi-Square	
	1970-71 1	1976-77 2	1980-81 3	1	2	3	1	2	3	1970-71 & 1976-77	1970-71 & 1980-81	1970-71 & 1976-77	1970-71 & 1980-81
M (Below 1)	37.63	42.39	19.21	5.67	6.32	5.1	15.07	14.91	26.55	0.23	0.17	0.002	20.221*
S (1-2)	18.91	18.15	19.41	9.36	9.61	8.7	49.50	52.95	44.82	0.14	0.14	0.240	0.442
SM (2-4)	20.44	18.53	27.98	20.00	19.76	19.4	97.85	106.64	69.34	0.20	0.22	0.790	8.307*
ME (4 -10)	18.01	16.84	26.20	38.11	38.08	38.8	211.60	226.13	148.09	0.28	0.30	0.998	19.062*
L. (10+)	5.01	4.00	7.20	26.86	26.23	28.0	516.17	655.75	388.89	0.15	0.17	37.744* NS	31.385* NS
All Sizes	100.00 (13754)**	100.00 (15038)**	100.00 (10271)	100.00 (39741)+	100.00 (41255)	100.00 (38900)	Weighted chi-square					6.133	16.381

Notes: 1 = 1970-71; 2 = 1976-77; and 3 = 1980-81
M = Marginal; S = Small; SM = Semi Medium; ME = Medium; L = Large
* Singnificant at 5% level. NS = Non-Significant
** = total in 100 holdings. + = area in 00' ha

Source: Statirtical abrtact of Punjab, different issues.

ICRs of the years 1970-71 and 1980-81 show that there is a decline in concentration ratios between size groups except marginal holdings. The increase in the concentration ratios of marginal holdings and decline in other classes except small holdings is significant. Weighted Chi-square indicates that the change has not been significant between these two periods.

From the above results it is clear that the interclass concentration is in favour of all holdings except marginal holdings in 1970-71 and 1976-77. The large land-holders with 10 hectares and above have gained significantly during the same time. But the results are altogether different for the periods 1970-71 and 1980-81. During the past decade, the lowest size owing below one hectare gained significantly. But a significant loss of share of land is noticed for all other groups. It is found that the weighted Chi-squares are not significant in both the sets of time periods. This may be due to the fact that average area of operational holdings of all 5 groups remained almost the same over the years under discussion indicating that no major shift in the pattern of distribution has taken place during 1970-71 to 1980-81.

Since land is a basic input of agricultural production, its skewed distribution affects the arrangement of other economic social and institutional factors. Limited access to land and its uneven distribution make less accessible other required inputs to come by. Prof. Frankel and Lipton are also of the view that resource-bias in favour of big farmers is one of the main factors leading to the widening of existing inequalities and poverty. Small farmers face difficulty in getting access to irrigation, credit and other technological inputs. Limited access to inputs (due to limited access to land) makes their agriculture less productive as compared with their large counterparts. To quote Prof. T.J. Byres:

> "The new strategy to the extent that new and reliable high yielding seeds can be provided to water-assured areas along with fertilisers and pesticides, creates profit possibilities of an unprecedented kind. These are, to be sure, limited to regions with assured irrigation, and within those regions the dice are heavily loaded in favour of rich peasants. The increase in working capital requirements brought about by the new seed-fertiliser-water-pesticide package is great and the new profit possibilities are, therefore, confined to those cultivators with large personal resource and/or access to credit on reasonable terms. Since peasants and share-croppers (who may be

one and the same) are excluded, because of lack of resources and lack of acceptable collateral."[20]

Let we discuss how far some of the inputs for agricultural development are biased towards rich farmers.

The success of green revolution in the Punjab mainly goes to tremendous expansion of irrigation base. At the time of re-organisation of the Punjab, the net area irrigated as percentage of net area sown was 59 per cent which increased to 84 per cent in 1979-80 and 91 per cent in 1987-88. During the past three decades the structure of area under irrigation has been changing in favour of tubewells. In 1960-61, 41 per cent of net area irrigated was under tubewells and wells which increased to 59 per cent in 1987-88. The number of tubewells (both diesel and electric operated) in Punjab was 1.92 lakhs in 1970-71 which increased to 5.85 lakhs in 1979-80 and 7.21 lakhs in 1987-88. Since tubewell is a capital intensive input and economically non-viable for a very small holding, it has been experienced that during the decade 1970-71 and 1980-81 the large farmers (with over 10 hectares of land) increased the irrigation base much faster than the small ones.

Table 3.7 shows the farm size and irrigation base for two agricultural censuses, i.e., 1970-71 and 1980-81. Table 3.7 clearly shows that the irrigation base of all the farm sizes has improved between the years of agricultural censuses. However, the percentage increase in irrigation base increases steeply as we move from small farm size to large farm size. The increase in irrigation base of the largest size (50+ hectares) is the highest, i.e., 102.60 per cent. The per cent increase in irrigation base in 1980-81 as compared with 1970-71 is in the range of 17 to 19 per cent for the farm sizes up to 10 hectares of land, but it is between 25 to 103 per cent for the farm sizes above 10 hectares. It is evident from Table 3.7 that there is a positive relationship between farm size and percentage increase in irrigation base in the years 1970-71 and 1980-81. Thus, it may be concluded that large farmers improve the irrigation base much faster than small farmers during the period under study.

Term credit is also very important for the cultivators to purchase the new inputs from the markets. Capital is being substituted for land and labour due to their limited availability. Since a sizeable chunk of the cultivators in the Punjab is marginal and small, the progress of these poor farmers depends upon acquiring of credit for purchasing the inputs. For example, Wills found in a study of Uttar Pradesh villages that small farmers could not use fertilisers along with HYV seeds because of credit constraint.[21] A number of studies[22] have concluded that the distribution of credit is more in favour of large farmers than small farmers. The available data[23] in Table 3.8 indicate that of the total credit advanced by both Primary Agricultural Credit Societies (PACS) and commercial banks, a larger proportion of term finance is usurped by the borrowers with holdings of above 2 hectares. The perusal of Table 3.8 shows that the amount of short-term loan per hectare from both PACS and commercial banks is lower on medium and large farmers having above two hectares of land than the small farmers with below two hectares of land. But the amount of credit per borrower is considerably higher on medium and large farmers than small farmers from both the financial institutions. It is also observed from Table 3.8 that primary agricultural credit societies cover only 48 per cent of the small farmers, whereas they serve all the farmers of over 2 hectares of land. On the other hand commercial banks cover only 5 per cent of the small farmers and 15 per cent of medium and large farmers. Thus the figures reveal the highly skewed distribution of institutional credit facilities in favour of the relatively large farmers. This biasedness is likely to generate adverse impact on the progress of poor farmers.

TABLE 3.7: Farm Size and Irrigation Base

Farm Size (ha)	Irrigation base		Percentage increase in 1980-81/1970-71
	1970-71	1980-81	
Below 1	69.5	81.7	17.55
1 - 2	71.5	84.1	17.62
2 - 3	72.7	85.6	17.74
3 - 4	73.6	87.4	18.75
4 - 5	74.3	86.9	16.95
5 - 7.5		86.9	
7.5 - 10	74.4	89.1	18.95*
10 - 20	70.6	87.9	24.50
20 - 30	62.5	85.5	36.80
30 - 40	57.5	88.7	54.26
40 - 50	55.1	91.5	66.06
50 +	38.5	78.0	102.60
All Sizes	71.7	86.89	21.19

Note: Irrigation base is net irrigated area as a percentage of net operated area.
* Calculated by taking the simple average of 1980-81 figure of two farm sizes.

Source: For 1970-71, Third Decenial Agricultural Census Report for Punjab, Chandigarh, Table 4.
For 1980-81, Report of Agricultural Census 1980-81, Pb.1985, Table 4.

TABLE 3.8: Distribution of Loans Advanced by PACS and Scheduled Commercial Banks by size of Holdings in Punjab, 1984-85

Size group of holdings	Primary agriculture credit societies			Scheduled commercial banks		
	Amount per Hec-atre (Rs)	Amount per borr-ower (Rs)	Percent-age of far-mers cov-ered	Amount per hect-are (Rs)	Amount per borr-ower (Rs)	Percentage of farmers covered
Below 2 hectares	1158	1831	48	140	2175	5
Above 2 hectares	435	3943	100	71	5135	15
Total	621	2751	90	86	4230	8

Source: T. Haque and Sunita Verma, *op. cit.*

Landless Labourers and Agricultural Wages

Apart from marginal and small farmers, there is high incidence of poverty among landless agricultural labourers. Despite green revolution and increase in money wages, they live in abject poverty. During the sixties, the Government adopted those policies of development where there was less risk of economic development. The various programmes started in 1960s look only those regions of various States for agricultural development where there was surety of increase in agricultural production. The programmes of subsidising new inputs and fixation of support prices encouraged agrarian capitalism in the country side. A number of studies[24] conducted in the heart land of green revolution concluded that the small farmers and agricultural labourers gained the least from the new technologies.

There was tremendous growth of agricultural labourers in the Punjab between the decenial census of 1961 and 1971. During this period landless agricultural labourers rose by 135.11 per cent. In 1961, 17.27 per cent of the total agricultural labourers were landless, but this figure increased to 32.09 per cent in 1971. The increase in landless agricultural labourers between 1971 and 1981 was 35.84 per cent. The large increase in the number of agricultural labourers between 1961 and 1971 may be due to

(i) the eviction of tenants from land due to land reform laws and green revolution;

(ii) the capitalist nature of new technology which is not afforded by poor farmers and they might have sold their land to join as wage-earners;
(iii) the increase in cost of living and monetisation of rural economy which forced the small farmers to hire out labour along with farming; and
(iv) high population growth in rural areas.

The Rural Labour Inquiry Report and the survey conducted in Punjab for the identification of weaker sections reveal that agricultural labour households constitute mostly scheduled caste households (about 85 per cent in 1964-65 and 1974-75). Due to poor economic and social status, the agricultural labourers are the depressed class in the rural society.

The landless labourers are dependent on wages. Therefore, their economic position can be well-judged by studying the trend of wages. This will also help in studying the impact of green revolution on the poorest section of the rural society. The trend of wages has been studied by dividing them into three categories, viz., the time before mid-sixties will be considered as pre-green revolution period; mid-sixties to early seventies as green revolution period and the period after early seventies as post-green revolution period. Table 3.9 gives operation-wise daily real wage rates for unskilled and skilled labourers for the period 1956 to 1988. In Table 3.9 money wages are deflated with the consumer Price Index for Agricultural Labourers by taking 1960-61 as base year.[25]

The figures in Table 3.9 show that there is erratic trend of wages in the Punjab. The overall tendency of the data for real wages is to increase. The perusal of Table 3.9 shows that the wages during harvesting time is generally higher than the other major operations of agriculture, e.g., ploughing and sowing. If we compare the real wages of different years between 1956 to 1965, i.e., pre-green revolution period, a slight fall in wages was observed in 1962, 1964 and 1965. The difference between the lowest and the highest wage rates was 17.10 per cent. Before 1965, the peak year for the wages was 1963. In the green revolution period (1966 to 1970), the lowest real wage was recorded in the year 1967 and the highest in 1970. There was a spurt in real wages in 1968. But after 1970 the wages continued to fall up to 1975. The sudden rise in wages in the latter half of sixties and early seventies may be due to increase in the demand for labour due to new agricultural strategy particularly its biological-chemical-water components. But the tendency of rising wages could not sustain for much of the years. In the post-green revolution period (1971 to 1988) the trend in wages was erratic. There was a fall in wages in the year 1971 and then rose up to 1974. After that the wages started rising up to 1980. The wages depressed again in the years 1981 and 1982. But, after 1984, there was an upward trend of wages in the Punjab. In 1984 the average real wage was only Rs. 2.90 which rose to Rs. 3.89 in 1988, i.e., an increase of 16.55 per cent. The harvesting wage increased by 34.40 per cent in the same period. A spurt in wages was recorded after 1984, except 1986-87 — a drought year.

TABLE 3.9: Real Wage Rates for Male Agricultural Labour in Punjab

(At constant prices: 1960-61)

Year	Ploughing	Sowing	Harvesting	Black Smith	Carpenter
1956	2.28	1.86	2.79	—	—
1957	2.36	2.08	3.23	—	—
1958	2.42	2.05	2.53	—	—
1959	2.46	2.12	2.30	—	—
1960	2.40	2.39	2.42	—	—
1961	2.50	2.49	2.59	4.24	4.41
1962	2.40	2.41	2.61	4.19	4.35
1963	2.67	2.91	2.69	4.43	4.47
1964	2.64	2.36	3.18	3.33	3.45
1965	2.48	2.45	2.88	3.93	3.93
1966	2.58	2.52	2.66	4.14	4.11
1967	2.20	2.15	2.54	3.62	3.66
1968	2.46	2.48	3.21	4.34	4.51
1969	3.19	3.17	3.85	5.28	5.28
1970	3.30	3.30	3.93	5.90	5.99
1971	3.25	3.25	3.89	6.03	6.03
1972	3.05	3.09	3.78	5.71	5.71
1973	2.94	2.98	3.70	5.73	5.36
1974	2.42	2.43	2.69	4.40	4.40
1975	2.56	2.61	3.14	4.46	4.46
1976	2.91	2.92	3.72	5.51	5.54
1977	2.83	2.83	2.82	5.67	5.74
1978	2.93	2.91	2.99	6.24	6.23
1979	2.95	3.04	2.85	6.28	6.27
1980	3.03	3.05	3.05	6.42	6.43
1981	2.49	2.78	2.68	5.65	5.65
1982	2.77	2.70	2.72	5.51	5.52
1983	2.89	2.89	2.93	6.18	6.22
1984	2.88	2.91	2.82	6.42	6.39
1985	3.06	3.30	3.79	7.21	7.19
1986	3.87	3.34	4.23	7.28	7.12
1987	3.31	3.31	4.13	—	—
1988	3.59	3.59	4.73	8.32	8.32

Source: Different Statistical Abstracts of Punjab.

The real wages for skilled labour of blacksmith and carpenters showed an upward tendency. While the periodic fluctuations are found in the wage rates of skilled labour, but these are lower than the real wage rates of agricultural operations.

The time trend has been fitted to the data given in Table 3.9. The values of intercept, co-efficients of time and coefficients of determination for different operations and periods are given in Table 3.10. The results of the Table 3.10 are interpreted as follows:

There is an increase in the real wages in the Punjab during 1956 and 1965. The coefficient of time for wages for ploughing and sowing are significant at 5 per cent level. The values of coefficient of determination (r^2) are 29 and 31 per cent. The significant increase in wages in the pre-green revolution period may be due to increase in production due to an increase in area under plough which increased the demand for labour and wages.

The green revolution period (1966-70) shows a positive trend in real wages of agricultural labourers. The coefficients of time for sowing and harvesting are positive and significant. It points to the fact that the green revolution has increased the demand for labour for all the three operations.

But this increase in wages could not continue for much of the time. There was an unprecedented fall in real wages between 1970-74. The coefficients of time in wages for this period are negative and significant. The fall in wages can be explained as follows:

(i) medium and large farmers who generally demand for hired labour started mechanising a few operations of agriculture, particularly after mid-sixties;

(ii) the in-flow of migrant labour from the neighbouring states increased the supply of labour; and

(iii) an increase in agricultural labourers for which the reasons have been mentioned above.

These are some of the reasons which increased the supply of labour and filled the gap between demand and supply of hired labour. It is evident from Table 3.10 that during 1971-84 the time trend for wages is negative for all the three agricultural operations, but the results are not significant.

TABLE 3.10: Time Trend in Wages in Different Periods in Punjab

Periods	Years (N)	Ploughing			Sowing			Harvesting		
		b_0	b_1	r^2	b_0	b_1	r^2	b_0	b_1	r^2
1956 - 65	10	2.3105	0.0290* (2.4377)	0.2870	1.8849	0.0773* (2.5590)	0.3148	2.6342	0.0156 (0.4116)	0.0004
1966 -70	5	2.0170	0.2430 (1.8214)	0.4164	1.9500	0.2580* (2.4976)	0.4794	2.8361	0.3660* (2.8881)	0.6922
1970 - 74	5	2.6280	-0.2070* (3.1100)	0.7353	2.6050	-0.2010* (2.7800)	0.6812	2.9607	-0.2670** (2.5100)	0.4506
1971 - 84	14	2.7779	-0.0111 (0.9989)	0.0419	2.9608	-0.0109 (1.8600)	0.0722	3.1265	-0.0210 (0.6037)	0.0143
1981 - 88	8	2.3467	0.1673* (2.7752)	0.4676	2.7013	0.0886 (1.0927)	0.0367	2.0178	0.3174* (5.7655)	0.8350

Figures in brackets are *t* - values.
* Significiant at 5 per cent level
** Significiant at 10 per cent level

The wages in 1980s show a positive and significant trend, except for sowing operation. The explanatory power of the trend lines is high. The increase in wages during this period may be due to a number of factors such as,

(i) the significant rise in the wages for harvesting operation may be due to the fact that in the recent years farmers have preferred non-mechanised harvesting to save hay. Because mechanised harvesting wastes the hay and the price of the same also increases a lot. Therefore, the mannual harvesting increased the demand for labour in the Punjab;

(ii) the violence in the Punjab affected the arrival and stay of migratory labour in the State, i.e., the supply of labour has gone down and

(iii) the increase in job opportunities by poverty alleviation programmes, viz., IRDP, RLEGP and NREP[26] has increased the demand for labour.

Thus the study of real wage rates shows that the condition of agricultural labourers has not improved much in the period under study. There was a spurt in real wages during the years 1968 and 1970. This increase in wages was mainly due to the compulsion of increase in demand for labour. But the increase in demand for labour was soon met by partly due to rising mechanisation and partly due to inflow of migrant labourers from the neighbouring States. Therefore, there was a significant fall in wages after 1970. The rise in wages after the year 1984 may be due to the impact of ongoing wage employment programmes and decline in inmigration of labour due to prevailing abnormal situations in the Punjab.

Wage Rates and Agricultural Production

There has been a considerable increase in production and productivity in the agriculture of Punjab. The question arises: Have the wages increased corresponding with the rise in production/productivity in agriculture? We hypothesize that there is a positive relationship between the wage rates and the productivity of land over the period under review. For analysis, the relationship between indices of agricultural wages and agricultural production (general) has been taken. The data for the period 1966 to 1985 have been considered here (see Table 3.11).

TABLE 3.11: Relationship of Agricultural Wages and General Agricultural Production.

Year	Indices of real wages	Indices of general agricultural production
1965-66	100	100
1966-67	89	113
1967-68	105	142
1968-69	132	158
1969-70	136	174
1970-71	134	182
1971-72	133	196
1972-73	129	193
1973-74	109	199
1974-75	102	206
1975-76	115	226
1976-77	110	237
1977-78	114	261
1978-79	116	293
1979-80	118	272
1980-81	107	276
1981-82	107	305
1982-83	114	318
1983-84	112	310
1984-85	131	353

Correlationship between wages and production: (1965-66 to 1974-75) = 0.5334^{NS}
Correlationship between wages and production: (1975-76 to 1984-85) = 0.6985*
* = significant at 5 per cent level.

The perusal of Table 3.11 shows that the indices of wages vary from 100 in 1965-66 to 131 in 1984-85, whereas the indices of production increase from 100 to 353 in the same period. The increase in indices both for wages and production is evident. In order to make the results more revealing, the coefficients of correlation between the indices of real wages and production for the periods 1966 to 1975 and 1976 to 1985 have been calculated. It is seen that coefficients of correlation for both the periods are positive. In the former period 28 per cent of the relationship is explained between the indices of real wages and agricultural production, whereas in the latter period 49 per cent of the relationship is explained. The coefficient of correlation is not significant for the former period, but significant at 5 per cent level for the latter period. Thus, we can say that with the rise in general agricultural production the real wage rates has also increased, but the increase in wages is comparatively less than the increase in production.

It points to the fact that agricultural development favoured more to the cultivators than the landless agricultural labourers. Therefore, the latter remained the weaker sections of the rural society.

Meagre Assets

Weaker sections of the society are deficient in assets. The asset structure of rural households indicates the extent of poverty in rural areas. Reserve Bank of India conducted two important surveys in 1961 and 1971 to find out the asset structure of rural households. In this analysis, the data pertaining to assets and distribution of assets in rural Punjab for the rural poor are obtained from All India Debt and Investment Survey (AIDIS), 1971-72. It studies the assets and liabilities of rural households as on 30th June 1971. In the report of Assets of Rural Households the definition of rural poor is given on the basis of value of assets. It is suggested that the households having assets less than Rs. 2,500 each may be taken as to represent the rural poor.[27]

This poor class of rural society comprises of cultivators who are only part-time farmers, as they have a very small parcel of land. They are mainly wage earners as their major source of income is earnings from farm and non-farm employment. There is not much difference between a part-time farmer and a labourer, except that the former personally cultivates a small piece of land. Similarly, artisans or village craftsman such as weavers, blacksmiths, potters, carpenters, etc., producing some traditional products for limited local market are also covered in this category. Since these traditional products are less in demand in the rural areas, many of them have to supplement their income from some kind of wage employment. The category 'other' non-cultivators includes unemployed persons, low paid village servants, people living on remittance from relatives etc., and wage earners depending on casual employment on some small local works.[28]

Table 3.12 shows the distribution of households according to asset groups in the Punjab in 1971. The data clearly show that 61 per cent of the cultivator households are in the last three asset groups and only 6 per cent are in the lowest asset groups. Top 61 per cent cultivator households usurp 91 per cent of the total assets of cultivating households. However, a large proportion of non-cultivators and its sub-groups are among the lowest three asset groups which are the rural poor according to RBI's survey. Among the sub-groups of non-cultivators, the economic condition of rural artisans is much better than agricultural labourers and 'other' non-cultivators. It is evident from Table 3.12 that there is heavy concentration of assets in the hands of wealthiest group in the rural areas.

TABLE 3.12: Percentage Distribution of Households According to Asset Groups and Share of Households in Each Asset Group in Total Value of Assets

(As on June, 1971)

Asset group (Rs.)	Cultivators		Agricultural labourers		Artisians		Other Non-cultivators		All non-cultivators	
	a	b	a	b	a	b	a	b	a	b
Up to 500	—	—	1.9	0.2	—	—	7.0	0.2	4.1	0.2
500 - 1000	0.3	—	7.6	1.9	2.1	0.2	8.0	0.4	7.3	0.7
1000 - 2500	1.5	0.1	36.2	17.9	29.9	8.5	19.3	2.4	27.9	5.6
2500 - 5000	4.5	0.3	39.6	39.8	32.4	19.5	20.0	5.4	30.0	12.6
5000 - 10000	8.5	1.0	12.1	23.0	24.5	28.8	17.6	8.5	15.7	12.4
10000 - 15000	7.2	1.5	2.7	17.2	11.1	43.0	28.1	83.2	15.1	68.5
15000 - 20000	4.9	1.4								
20000 - 30000	12.4	4.9								
30000 - 50000	16.8	10.6								
50000 - 100000	26.1	29.1								
100000+	17.9	51.2								
Over all:	100	100	100	100	100	100	100	100	100	100
Gini-Ratio:	0.4818		0.3837		0.4854		0.7003			

Note: a = Proportion of households.
b = Share of total assets owned.
Source: R.B.I's Survey (1971), *op. cit*

In the Punjab a sizeable proportion (23.2%) of total households is in the three lowest asset groups, i.e., rural poor. Of the total households having assets below Rs. 2500 each, the majority of them are non-cultivators. Only 3.3 per cent cultivators and 96.7 per cent non-cultivator households are rural poor. It is also found that the poverty is largely concentrated in agricultural labourers and 'other' non-cultivators.

The above discussion points to the existence of inequality in the household assets by different classes of rural households. As the proportion of households in various asset groups and the proportion of assets held by them differ among different classes of households, a measure is required for objectively showing the inequality of distribution of assets. The Gini's ratio (GR) is calculated here. There are certain limitations of GR for interpreting the results. For example, the Gini ratio represents the overall pattern of distribution of households and the share of assets held by them — a number of different distribution pattern may give an identical GR values. Moreover, the degree of inequality may differ over different segments of the Lorenz Curves yielding even the same overall Gini ratio. Despite these limitations the results of Gini ratios are widely interpreted. In Table 3.12, there is less inequality among agricultural labour households and high in 'other' non-cultivators. The highest GR in 'other' non-cultivators may be due to the fact that this group comprises of heterogeneous elements, such as moneylenders, traders, professionals etc.

Composition of Assets

In the Punjab, land is the most important asset with the cultivators which accounts for 77 per cent of the total assets. The next important item is buildings forming about 10 per cent of the total assets while the livestock and implements and machinery record 4.8 and 4 per cent respectively. In case of agricultural labourers and artisans, the most important asset is buildings which accounts for about 54 and 66 per cent of the total assets respectively. Livestock is more important with agricultural labourers than other groups. Durable household assets are the third most important item with the agricultural labourers. The land is the most important asset for 'other' non-cultivators. It is mainly due to the fact that land is kept by moneylenders, traders, professionals etc.

Table 3.13 presents the average value of assets per household. The average value of total assets per household among the cultivating households is the highest. It may be due to the fact that new agricultural strategy has substantially increased the yield of the farmers, particularly, the large farmers due to higher irrigation facilities and productivity of land. It is seen that 33 per cent of the large farmers (with over 10 acres of land) operate 67 per cent of land. They are in a position to reap larger benefit from new agricultural technologies.

Table 3.13 shows that the difference between the average value of total assets held by a cultivator household and an agricultural labour household is considerably wider than between a cultivator and 'other' non-cultivator household. The average value of assets for agricultural labour households is only one-eighteenth of the average value of assets of cultivator households in Punjab. It shows that there is a large divergence in the economic condition of cultivators and agricultural labourers. This indicates the concentration of poverty among agricultural labourers and the prosperity of cultivators.

TABLE 3.13: Composition of Assets of Different Households

Items	Cultivators	Agricultural labourers	Artisans	Other Non-cultivators
Land	77.3	8.7	2.9	57.1
Vacant Land for House Site	0.9	2.4	0.5	1.3
Buildings	9.9	53.9	66.9	26.2
Livestock	4.8	19.1	9.8	4.2
Implements & machinery	4.0	2.1	7.5	1.2
Durable Household assets	2.1	12.4	9.9	5.4
Financial assets:				
(i) Share	0.1	0.4	0.4	0.2
(ii) Deposits	0.5	0.8	1.2	4.0
Dues receivable:				
(i) Cash	0.4	0.2	0.3	0.4
(ii) Kind	0.1	-	0.1	—
Overall:	100.0	100.0	100.0	100.00
Average value of assets per H.H(Rs)	62,789	3,473	6,096	14,045

Source: As in Table 3.12

In Tables 3.12 and 3.13, it is clear that the economic position of artisans as a class is better than that of agricultural labourers in Punjab. The average value of total assets of an artisan household is 1.75 times more than an agricultural labour household. But an average artisan household owns one-tenth of the assets of a cultivator household in Punjab.

The above discussion shows that the concentration of assets is in favour of cultivator households. The rural poor in Punjab comprises of part-time cultivators, landless labourers and poor artisans and 'other' non-cultivators. There is a need to improve the level of assets of these classes. The improvement in the assets of poor people will certainly reduce the high concentration of the asset distribution among the richest classes.

Pattern of Assets of Rural Poor

RBI's survey indicates that in Punjab 23.2 per cent or about 3.58 lakh households were poor in the year 1971, i.e., their owned total assets were lower than Rs. 2,500 each. Among these households, only 3 per cent were cultivators, 51 per cent landless labourers, 39 per cent 'other' non-cultivators and 7 per cent artisans. It clearly indicates that agricultural labourers in the rural society are under the yoke of poverty and are rightly called as the unprivileged class of the rural society. The composition of assets of rural poor is presented in Table 3.14.

TABLE 3.14: Asset Holdings of Rural Households in the Asset Group below Rs.2,500 in the Punjab

(As on 30-6-1971)

Assets	Proportion of H.H. Reporting (%)	Average Value per H.H. (Rs.)	Proportion to total assets
Land	1.1	9	0.6
Vacant land for house site	15.8	40	2.8
Buildings	84.2	771	54.1
Livestock	61.5	242	16.9
Implements & machinery	60.4	55	3.9
Durable Household assets	99.2	268	18.8
Financial assets:			
(i) Shares	16.3	9	0.6
(ii) Deposits	6.8	25	1.8
Receivable:			
(i) Cash	3.5	7	0.5
(ii) Kind	—	—	—
Overall:	99.7.	1426	100.0

Source: As in Table 3.12

The perusal of Table 3.14 shows that 99.7 per cent of the poor households report one form or another form of asset. The average value of assets held per household in this group is only Rs. 1,426. These poor households constitute 23 per cent of the sample households, and they shared only one per cent of the total assets of rural households. Out of this meagre average value of Rs. 1,426 per household, more than 50 per cent, i.e., Rs. 771 of the value of assets is taken by a single item, buildings. The other important assets are livestock and durable household assets.

The poverty of these households is further illustrated by the proportion of households reporting about these assets. It is observed from Table 3.14 that 38 per cent of the total rural poor households have no livestock which is a productive asset. As many as 16 per cent of the households have no house of their own in 1971 in Punjab. Ownership of land is not reported by as many as 99 per cent of the poor households. It gives us the impression that the most of the poor households are landless.

NOTES

1. P.K. Bardhan, 'The Pattern of Income Distribution in India; A Review', *Sankhya: The Indian Journal of Statistics*, Vol. 36, 1974, pp. 103-38.
2. (a) C.K. Johri and B.K. Jain, 'The structure of Indian Poverty', An ICSSR's Project.
   (b) Dandekar and Rath, *Poverty in India*, Indian School of Political Economy, Bombay.
3. There is wide variation in the estimates of people below poverty line. For example, according to NSS data there were only 12 per cent rural people below poverty line, whereas Weaker Section Survey estimated roughly 31 per cent of the rural population below poverty line in Punjab.
4. Gadgil group consisted of D.R. Gadgil, P.S. Loknathan, M.R. Masani, Ashok Mehta, Shriman Naryan, Pitamber Pant, V.K.R.V. Rao and Anna Sahib Sahas.
5. B.S. Minhas, 'Rural Poverty, Land Redistribution and Development', *Indian Economic Review*, April 1970.
6. A.Vaidyanathan, 'Some Aspects of Inequality in Living Standards in Rural India', in Srinivasan and Bardhan (ed)., *Poverty and Income Distribution in India*, 1974.
7. M.S. Ahluwalia, 'Rural Poverty in India: 1956-57 to 1973-74', World Bank Staff Working Paper No. 279, p. 11.
8. Bhanwar Singh, *Agrarian Structure, Technological Change and Poverty*, Agricole Publishing Academy, 1985, p. 19.
9. (a) M.S. Ahluwalia, 'Rural Poverty and Agricultural Performance in India', *Journal of Development Studies*, April, 1978.
   (b) C.K. Johri & B.K. Jain: *op. cit.*
   (c) P.K. Bardhan, 'On the Incidence of Poverty in Rural India of the sixties', *EPW*, February, 1973.
   (d) I. Rajaramana, 'Poverty, Inequality and Economic Growth in Rural India, 1960-61 to 1970-71, *Journal of Development Studies*, July 1974.
10. It is mentioned here that NSSO did not conduct consumer expenditure survey'for two year viz. 1962-63 and 1971-72. We have interpolated the data for those years for the purpose of fitting a time trend line.
11. Gunvant M. Desai, 'Trends in Rural Poverty in India', in Mellor and Desai (ed.), *Agricultural Change and Rural Poverty*, Oxford University Press, New Delhi, 1986, p. 6.
12. These words of Prof. Dharam Narain are quoted from G.M. Desai '*Trends in Rural Poverty in India*', Mellor and Desai (ed.), *op. cit.* p. 2.
13. The Consumer Price Index for agricultural labourers increased by 50 per cent during 1960-61 and 1966-67.
14. 'Bardhan (1982) argues that there was some growth in real net value added in agriculture per capita in some States, such as Punjab and Haryana, but the extent

of poverty in these States has not declined significantly, whether this contradicts the trickle-down hypothesis depends on its precise specification. One could argue that not only does the growth in income per capita have to be substantial but it has to be sustained for a sufficiently long period for the trickle down process to operate. Also, migration into Punjab and Haryana could have slowed the trickle-down process'.

T.N. Srinivasan, '*Agriculture Production, Relative Prices and Poverty*', in Mellor and Desai (ed.), *op. cit*., p. 51.

15. P.K. Bardhan, 'Poverty and 'Trickle-Down' in Rural India', in Mellor and Desai (ed.), *op. cit*. p. 79.
16. A study by Oberai and Singh (1980) did not confirm this conclusion. They undertook a survey of 2124 households in 26 villages in Ludhiana, Punjab, in 1977. They found that there were 92 agricultural labourers in-migrants and 79 out-migrants so there was net in-migration of only 13 agricultural labourers in the whole sample.

    A.S. Oberai and H.K. Manmohan Singh, 'Migration Flows in Punjab's Green Revolution Belt', *EPW*, March 29, 1980.
17. The data were published in *Sarvekshna*, Vol. IV, No. 1 & 2 (July-Oct. 1980), Government of India, Delhi.
18. C.T. Kurien, *Dynamics of Rural Transformation: A Study of Tamil Nadu: 1950-75*, Orient Longman Ltd. 1981, p. 10.
19. The procedure for calculation of weights is given in C.T. Kurien, *op. cit*.
20. T.J. Byres, 'The Dialectic of India's Green Revolution', *South Asian Review*, Vol. 5, January 1972, p. 104.
21. I.R. Wills, 'Green Revolution and Agricultural Employment and Income in Western U.P', *EPW*, March 27, 1971.
22. (a) C.H.H. Rao, *Technological Change and Distribution of Gains in Indian Agriculture*, Macmillan & Co.

    (b) M. Lipton, 'Inter-farm, Inter-regional and farm and non-farm Income Distribution', *World Development*, Vol. 6, 1978.
23. T. Haque and S. Verma, 'Regional and Class Disparities in the Flow of Agricultural Credit', *IJAE*, Vol. 43, July-Sep. 1988.
24. (a) E.J. Clay, 'Equity and Productivity Effects of a Package of Technical Innovations and Changes in Social Situations, tube-wells, tractors and HYVs', *IJAE*, Oct.-Dec., 1975.

    (b) A.V. Jose, 'Trends in Real Wage Rates of Agricultural labour', *EPW*, Sept. 1971.

    (c) R.K. Mahajan, 'Dynamics of Agriculture and Wages of Agricultural Labourers', *MDU Research Journal* (Arts), Oct. 1987.
25. The data for Consumer Price Indices for Agricultural Labourers are obtained from the various issues of *Agricultural Situation in India*, Ministry of Agriculture and Rural Development, Government of India, New Delhi.
26. In Punjab RLEGP and NREP generated employment of 19.57 and 17.65 lakh mandays, respectively during 1987-88. The generation of employment was much higher in 1985-86 and 1986-87.
27. RBI. *All India Debt and Investment Survey (1971-72), Assets of Rural Households as on June 30, 1971*, Bombay, 1976, p. 132.
28. *Ibid*., pp. 132-33.

FOUR

INTEGRATED RURAL DEVELOPMENT PROGRAMME IN PUNJAB: An Appraisal

THE INTEGRATED Rural Development Programme (IRDP) was launched in a modest scale during 1978-79 and extended to all the blocks of the country in 1980. This has been the single most important programme of poverty alleviation in the rural society since 1978. A few programmes were started after the year 1970 for the benefit of the target groups, i.e., small and marginal farmers and agricultural labourers, and backward areas. But these programmes contributed little towards the income and employment of the rural poor in general. Moreover the earlier programmes were segmented and cater to the agricultural development only. The IRDP is a multi-sectoral, systematic and well-conceived programme for improving the social and economic life of a specific group of people. The target groups consist of small and marginal farmers, agricultural and non-agricultural labourers, rural artisans and craftsmen, scheduled castes and scheduled tribes. The programme is to identify families below the poverty line (based on income criteria) and to formulate projects for them in primary, secondary and tertiary sectors. The thrust of the programme is in generating opportunities for employment by giving them productive assets and resources.

The economy of Punjab is predominantly agrarian. The tremendous break-through in agriculture after 1966 has decidedly improved the quality of life of rural poor, but, at the same time, it has accentuated inequalities among different rural classes. The percolation of the gains of agricultural technology to the small and marginal farmers and labourers, who were largely lacking resources and skills, was a thin trickle. Therefore, there was a need of the programme which could provide assets and/or skills, self and/or wage employment and income to the target people. The IRDP aims at helping the target groups. Like the other States of Indian Union, the Punjab initiated the IRD programme in 1978-79 covering a few blocks under the control of Development Department of the State. From 2nd October, 1980 all other agencies were merged into the new programme of IRD and it was extended to all the blocks in the State. This programme has attracted the maximum public attention as compared to other developmental programmes introduced in the State. A number of studies have been conducted by Government, institutions and individuals for the evaluation of the programme. Majority of the studies are critical of the malpractices, corruption and inefficiencies involved in the implementation of the programme in the State. We shall like to seek answers to a few questions which are generally asked for the programme. These are: What proportion of rural poor are misclassified? What kind of assets the beneficiaries received out of the financial assistance given under the programme? Do the assets remain with the beneficiaries? Does the programme generate sufficient income to enable the beneficiaries to cross the poverty line? In other words, we try to assess the programme and its viability.

Our analysis and discussion of the various issues are based on the secondary data generated by Government agencies, individual researchers and different research institutions. The results will be further supported by the primary data collected by the author from five villages of three districts viz., Gurdaspur, Ludhiana and Faridkot of Punjab. The samples of sixty beneficiary households and equal number of non-beneficiary households were taken. The study was conducted in the year 1985-86.

Objectives of the Programme

The main objective of the IRDP is to evolve an operationally integrated strategy for the purpose of increasing production and productivity in agriculture and allied sectors for the resource and income development of target group of the population in all the blocks of the State. It is found that the poor people remain poor because they mostly do not possess any productive asset other than their labour. Therefore, any development strategy which aims at improving the lot of rural poor must intend to create productive assets for them. For this the viable economic activities started under this programme can help the target households. There can be improvement in the productivity of land of small and marginal farmers by providing them access to inputs such as water, improved seeds and fertilisers etc. The diversification of agriculture through animal husbandry, dairy, forestry, fishery etc. will benefit both landless and land-owners. Small-scale and cottage industries based on local resources will also have to be identified and fully exploited. There is need to promote the tertiary activities such as repair-shops, a small business, knitting and sewing etc.

Scope and Coverage

When the programme was started during 1978-79, initially a cluster of five contiguous villages in each of 117 blocks in the State was taken for planning and development. In each focal point certain rural infrastructural facilities were proposed to be provided to achieve integration of agricultural and non-agricultural activities. However, in 1980 the Sixth Five Year Plan was recast and the IRD programme was extended to all the blocks. Its coverage was not confined to a cluster of villages alone but to all the villages in the State. IRDP is a comprehensive programme of reducing poverty in the rural areas. It is proposed to uplift at least 600 families of target groups (of which at least 50 per cent should belong to scheduled castes and scheduled tribes) in each block everywhere. Of these, approximately 400 families were expected to benefit through agriculture and related activities, about hundred families through village and cottage industries and the remaining hundred families assisted in the services sector.

An Appraisal of IRD Programme

IRD programme is designed to develop self-employment ventures in the activities pertaining to primary, secondary and tertiary sectors. In order to diversify the occupational structure in the rural economy, it is decided to assist about 33 per cent of the beneficiaries under secondary and tertiary sector activities in Punjab. The assets provided to the beneficiaries are financed partly by the Government and partly by the credit institutions. Generally subsidy part is given by the Government and loans by the bank. The capital cost of the asset is subsidised at the rate of 25 per cent to small farmers and 33.33 per cent to marginal farmers, agricultural and non-agricultural labourers and scheduled castes. However, the maximum amount of subsidy is fixed at Rs. 3000 for all the categories except scheduled tribes.

TABLE 4.1: Total Investment and Number of Beneficiaries under the IRDP: Punjab (Sixth Plan)

Items/Years	1980-81	1981-82	1982-83	1983-84	1984-85	1980-85	1985-86	1986-87	1987-88
1	2	3	4	5	6	7	8	9	10
1. Total govt. expenditure (subsidy Rs. Lakh)	564.48 (34.86)	646.15 (36.44)	872.55 (31.92)	766.65 (32.71)	865.52 (32.70)	3715.35 (33.42)	737.15 (30.21)	1250.33 (29.52)	828.72 (27.91)
2. Total term credit advanced by all banks (Rs. Lakh)	1054.84 (65.14)	1127.07 (63.56)	1860.94 (68.08)	1577.37 (67.29)	1781.52 (67.30)	7402.71 (66.58)	1703.36 (69.79)	2985.92 (70.48)	2141.58 (72.09)
3. Total investment (1+2)	1619.32 (100.00)	1773.22 (100.00)	2733.49 (100.00)	2344.02 (100.00)	2647.04 (100.00)	11118.06 (100.00)	2440.51 (100.00)	4236.23 (100.00)	2970.30 (100.00)
4. Total beneficiaries	63361	86867	98436	72963	74136	395762	64612	99935	74367
5. Scheduled caste beneficiaries	26,796 (42.29)	39931 (45.97)	52581 (53.42)	41235 (46.57)	41606 (56.12)	202149 (51.08)	32379 (50.11)	53035 (53.07)	39056 (52.52)
6. Subsidy per beneficiary (Rs.)	890.90	743.84	886.41	1050.74	1167.48	938.78	1140.89	1251.14	1114.37
7. Credit per beneficiary (Rs.)	1664.81	1297.47	1890.51	2161.88	2403.04	1870.49	2636.19	2987.84	2879.75
8. Investment per beneficiary (Rs.)	2555.71	2041.31	2776.92	3212.62	3570.52	2809.27	3777.18	4238.98	3994.12
9. Subsidy-credit ratio	1 : 1.9	1 : 1.7	1 : 2.1	1 : 2.1	1 : 2.1	1 : 2	1 : 2.3	1 : 2.4	1:2.6
10. Beneficiaries per block in a year	537	736	834	618	628	671	548	847	630

Note: Figures in parentheses are percentage to total.
Source: Different Annual Plans of Punjab.

The scale and composition of assistance provided under IRDP in Punjab during Sixth Plan (1980-85) and up to 1987-88 is given in Table 4.1. The perusal of Table 4.1 shows that total term credit advanced by different credit institutions in different years is increasing. In 1980-81, per beneficiary capital investment (subsidy + loan) was about Rs. 2,556 which increased to Rs. 3,571 in 1984-85 and Rs. 3,994 in 1987-88. The share of subsidy in the total credit has decreased from about 36 per cent in 1981-82 to only 28 per cent in 1987-88. This result is further supported by the fact that subsidy-credit ratio is improving. On an average, during Sixth Plan this ratio was 1 : 2. It means that total subsidy was one-third of the total capital investment. But after 1984-85 this ratio has started improving, i.e., the proportion of loan part is increasing more than before.

In the guidelines to the Rural Development Agency, (Punjab), it is envisaged that on an average six hundred families are to be assisted under the IRDP. Out of these assisted families 30 per cent weightage should be given to scheduled castes and scheduled tribes. However, in Punjab, the proportion of scheduled caste beneficiaries are about 50 per cent against the target of 30 per cent as laid down by the circular of Rural Development Ministry. But in actual sense, the proportion of scheduled caste beneficiaries is more than even the 50 per cent of the total beneficiaries. The perusal of Table 4.1 shows that out of the total beneficiaries, 51 to 57 per cent of the scheduled castes beneficiaries are actually assisted in different years after 1982-83. The number of beneficiaries per block assisted in different years have also not uniform pattern. During the Sixth Plan period, the number of beneficiaries per block were well-above the target limit of 600 except in the year 1980-81. After that there were only 548 beneficiaries per block in 1985-86, 847 in 1986-87 and 630 in 1987-88 which were assisted under the programme.

A major drawback of the programme is that it allocates the same number of beneficiaries in each block irrespective of the number of households below poverty line in them. As we know that there exists a wide economic inequalities in different districts of Punjab mainly due to factor-endowment. It is generally felt that green revolution has further accentuated these inequalities. Therefore, if the allocation of beneficiaries per block is uniform, then it is possible that some of the ineligible families may also be selected. There is also a fear that the district having more poor households may continue to stay in the same position because of less proportion of households has been assisted there than the district where the number of people below poverty line are less.

Block Plan

The IRD is an umbrella programme conceived as an anti-poverty programme. Therefore, the strategy and implementation of the programme must be foolproof. The Ministry of Rural Development, Government of India, has directed the States to prepare a five year perspective plan for each block and aggregate the plans at the district level. This plan must be based on practical possibilities of development in primary, secondary and tertiary sectors. Block level planning is done in two stages: (i) Five Year Perspective Plan; and (ii) An annual Action Plan. This plan is based on an assessment of developmental assets of the block and deals with optimum utilisation of resources. The formulation of a perspective block plan is an important dimension of IRDP. This is necessary for the proper implementation of the programme and for reaching poorest of the poor households. The resource inventory of block/district plan concentrates on indentifying the potentialities which can be best exploited at the block/district level. Despite the importance of these block plans, they are not being prepared as the guidelines given by the Ministry of Rural Development. When the attention of some officials of DRDAs were drawn towards the non-formulation of block plans, they held non-availability of requisite manpower and expertise responsible for the same. Similarly the guidelines to prepare district plans are not adhered to resulting into improper planning at district level.

Identification of Target Groups

The first most important task of the programme is to identify the target group households. The Ministry of Rural Development has laid down certain norms regarding the identification of poor people. According to the guidelines, all those households with a total annual income of less than Rs. 3,500 or an annual per capita income less than Rs. 700 in the year 1979-80 would be treated as poor or below the poverty line. This identification of poor households will be done on the basis of State wide survey specially conducted for this purpose. But no such household-survey in the Punjab, according to the guidelines provided, was conducted before giving the benefit schemes to the beneficiaries.

The Weaker Section Survey conducted in the Punjab by the Economic and Statistical Organisation, Punjab, in October, 1980 was made the base for the identification of the target families for the IRD Programme. It is found that all those households having annual income below Rs. 3,600, according to the survey, have been issued yellow cards for their identification. Accordingly, the survey revealed that 7.44 Lakh families were living below the poverty line in the rural areas of Punjab in the year 1980. It is decided that only those families holding yellow cards would be covered under the benefit schemes of the programme. These target families consist of mostly landless labourers, small and marginal farmers, petty shop-keepers, artisans, scheduled castes etc. During the Seventh Five Year Plan, IRDP will cover the household whose annual income is up to Rs. 4,800 as against the coverage of families having annual income of Rs. 3,500 during the Sixth Plan.

Before discussing the case of misclassification of poor households in the State, we raise certain doubts about the survey conducted for the identification of the people below the poverty line. First, the purpose of the Weaker Section Survey was limited. It might not be as serious as the identification of the people below the poverty line. Secondly, the identification of target groups made on the basis of above survey violated the minimum norm of annual income of Rs. 3,500. Thirdly, the survey was conducted by the single institution with the help of less trained Government personnels and without the involvement of the agencies and people at the grass-root level. Even the involvement of banks which had to provide finance to the schemes in the identification of the beneficiaries was not there. Fourthly, as per official guidelines, the list of identified potential beneficiaries prepared by the officials has to be presented in the *Gram Sabha* meeting for the approval of target households before the beneficiaries were actually assisted. These checks were involved to ensure that the most deserving poor households get the benefit of the scheme. But this procedure was not adopted in Punjab, strictly according to the guidelines.

A number of evaluation studies[1] of IRDP have reported about the misclassification of the poor households in different parts of the country and the Punjab is no exception. A few studies presented below give details of the misclassification of the target groups in Punjab.

A NABARD (1984)[2] study brought to light that 35 per cent of the total beneficiaries were misclassified in Punjab.

Programme Evaluation Organisation of Planning Commission

(1985),[3] on the basis of sample households of Ferozepur and Sangrur districts of Punjab, reported that 35 per cent and 21 per cent of the total beneficiary households were non-poor in the two districts respectively.

The primary sample survey conducted by the author (1988)[4] in the year 1986 found that 32 per cent beneficiary households (when the poverty line cut-off point was taken as Rs. 4,800 per year) and 52 per cent persons on the basis of per capita income of Rs. 960 per annum, were actually below the poverty line. It means that 68 per cent of the beneficiary households received subsidies and bank loans but they were non-poor according to the definition given above.

Concurrent Evaluation Survey of IRDP is carried out by 29 reputed research institutions in the country on behalf of the Government of India. During 1985-86 the survey generated a lot of data for the evaluation of this programme. In this survey all the districts in the country were covered on a rotation basis. From each district a sample of 40 IRDP beneficiaries was studied in detail. This study shows that if the poverty line in Punjab is defined as Rs. 3,500 per annum then 49 per cent of the total beneficiaries will be non-poor at the time of assistance. But when Rs. 4,800 is considered to be the cut-off point as shown in the Seventh Plan, the misclassification of beneficiary households decreased to only 9 per cent of the total sample beneficiaries.[5]

Table 4.2 clearly shows that the beneficiaries of the programme in Punjab are not selected on the *Antyodaya* principle. Therefore, it may be possible that the households in the range of income of Rs. 2,266 to Rs. 4,800 got more benefit of the scheme than the destitutes with the income less than Rs. 2,266 per annum.

TABLE 4.2: Distribution of Income at the Time of Assistance in Punjab

(Percentages)

Household Income (Rs)	Per cent Households
1-2265	12
2266-3500	39
3501-4800	40
4801-6400	7
6401+	2
Total	100

Source: N.J. Kurian, *op. cit.*

Thus the above-mentioned studies clearly indicate the misclassification of target households. There exists a wide variation in the cut-off point of the poverty line and estimates of misclassification of the target households. Therefore, roughly 35 to 40 per cent of the households in Punjab may be misclassified. Such wrong identification of the households will certainly encourage malpractices and corruption. The percentage of non-poor beneficiaries can be minimised, if not reduced to zero, by being utmost careful at the time of identification of target families by the involvement of different rural based institutions in the survey for identification of people below the poverty line. *Antyodaya* principle in the selection of the beneficiaries is also not being strictly followed in the State.

Benefit Schemes

The selection of schemes under the programme has shown an overwhelming bias towards animal husbandry, more particularly milch cattle.[6] According to the guidelines of IRDP the assistance can be provided to beneficiaries to take-up economic activities under various schemes of the programme. All these activities have been divided into three sectors, viz., primary, secondary and tertiary sectors.

In case of the Punjab, it is targeted to cover atleast 600 poor households per block per annum for the implementation of IRDP. It is proposed to cover 400 families (67%) under primary sector and hundred (17%) each under secondary and tertiary sector schemes. The field experience shows that the Government officials preferred to provide assistance to only those schemes which are manageable to the officials of the programme. In this process they least bother about the preference of the beneficiaries, income generating potential of the asset, infrastructure available with the beneficiary households, marketing of the product produced by the assets etc. In the field study, we have observed that in some of the villages almost all the beneficiaries were given milch animals. It resulted into the decrease of price of milk in that area mainly because of its excess supply. This way the basic purpose of the whole programme is defeated.

The figures regarding sectoral distribution of beneficiaries who have taken different schemes of IRDP in the Punjab from 1980-81 to 1984-85 are given in Table 4.3. During the Sixth Plan period, 56 per cent of the beneficiaries received assets in the primary sector as compared to 8 per cent in secondary sector and 36 per cent in tertiary sector in the Sate. But if we show dry animals/animal carts in primary sector activities and recast Table 4.3 accordingly then a different picture will emerge. It is mainly because of the fact that dry animals such as bullocks, camels etc. and animal carts are purchased mainly for agriculture. In the revised Table 4.4, we find that the primary sector schemes show over 67 per cent share in the total schemes assisted under the programme. Table 4.4 presents activity-wise number of assisted beneficiaries. It is evident from Table 4.4 that out of total schemes adopted by the beneficiaries, the activities concerning animal husbandry are very popular with the beneficiary households. Among animal husbandry schemes, dairy farming is the most important activity. That is why IRDP is sometimes called a 'cow-buffalo' programme in Punjab. It appears that the total thrust of the programme imagination has come to rest on just on the purchase of livestock.[7] Though the sub-sector of animal husbandry under IRDP has been the subject of criticism over the years, yet this sub-sector is given priority under the programme. In Punjab during the years 1980-81 and 1981-82, the share of animal husbandry activity with the assisted beneficiaries was about 43 per cent and 45 per cent respectively, whereas its share increased to 54 to 64 per cent in the subsequent years.

TABLE 4.3: Sectorwise Distribution of Beneficiaries Assisted in Punjab from 1980-81 to 1984-85

Year	Beneficiaries Assisted Under			
	Primary sector	Secondary sector	Tertiary sector	Total
1	2	3	4	5
1980-81	43,234 (68.23)	5,277 (8.33)	14,850 (23.44)	63,361 (100.00)
1981-82	56,897 (65.50)	3,749 (4.32)	26,221 (30.18)	86,867 (100.00)
1982-83	53,918 (54.78)	8,037 (8.16)	36,480 (37.06)	98,435 (100.00)
1983-84	37692 (51.66)	6,198 (7.12)	30,073 (41.22)	72,963 (100.00)
1984-85	28,957 (39.06)	10,180 (13.73)	34,999 (47.21)	74,136 (100.00)
Sixth Plan (1980-85)	220698 (55.76)	32441 (8.20)	142623 (36.04)	39576 (100.00)

Note: Figures in brackets indicate percentage to total.
Source: The Secretary Rural Development and Panchayats, Punjab.

TABLE 4.4: Activity-wise Number of Assisted Beneficiaries

(Percentages)

Activity	1980-81	1981-82	1982-83	1983-84	1984-85	(Sixth Plan Period) (1980-85)
1. Agriculture	35.05	26.78	4.24	0.02	—	12.63
2. Pumpsets	2.02	1.37	0.46	0.20	—	0.77
3. Animal husbandry	42.51	45.27	61.60	63.75	53.91	53.84
(a) Dairying	29.69	35.62	47.77	49.23	36.08	40.29
(b) Others	12.82	9.65	13.83	14.52	17.83	13.55
Total (1+2+3)	79.58	73.42	65.30	63.97	53.91	67.24
4. Secondary	8.33	4.32	8.16	7.12	13.73	8.20
5. Tertiary	12.09	22.26	26.54	28.91	32.36	24.56
Grand Total	100.00 (63361)	100.00 (86867)	100.00 (98435)	100.00 (72963)	100.00 (74136)	100.00 (395762)

Note: (a) Figures in parentheses show the total number of beneficiaries assisted.
(b) Animal husbandry includes milch animals, poultry, sheep/goat/piggery and animal carts.
(c) Secondary sector includes the beneficiaries assisted under Rural Industries, workshops and sericulture.
(d) Tertiary Sector consists of the schemes such as sewing/knitting machines, small business and services and others.

Source: Same as in Table 4.3.

The persual of Table 4.4 shows that agriculture and pumpsets which accounted for 35 per cent and 2 per cent of the total schemes, respectively, in the year 1980-81 had been dropped for assistance since the year 1984-85. In fact, it was decided in a meeting of all the Project Officers, of all the District Rural Development Agencies and State level Co-ordination Committee in February 1982 that subsidy on the supply of agricultural implements should be stopped. This resulted into less weightage of agricultural and allied activities and pumpsets, but non-farm activities received more attention of the beneficiaries. A close look on Table 4.4 reveals that with the withdrawal of subsidy on the schemes, the beneficiaries preferred to opt for animal husbandry and tertiary sector activities.

During the Sixth Five Year Plan (1980-85), the main position was occupied by dairy farming under primary sector. This single activity accounted for 40 per cent of the total beneficiaries in Punjab. That is why about 9 per cent of the total beneficiaries opted the activities under this sector. Any how, the position of beneficiaries for adopting tertiary sector schemes was better than secondary sector schemes.[8]

Status of the Asset

A number of studies[9] conducted in the field have reported that the asset provided under IRDP to some of the beneficiaries has disappeared. Either the asset is not actually received and is merely shown in the official record or after acquiring the asset it has been sold to some other person. In this way a single asset is sold to so many beneficiaries with the help of intermediaries and officials. It is in this context that 'IRDP Cow' is known as ' Circulating Capital'.[10]

We report here the findings of a survey conducted in the three districts of Punjab, viz. Gurdaspur, Ludhiana and Faridkot by the author. The results are shown in Table 4.5. Table 4.5 shows that 85 per cent of the selected beneficiaries in the Punjab have the asset intact with them at the time of survey. The remaining 15 per cent of the assets were either sold to some body else or reported the death of the animals. It is observed that almost all the assets reported to be not intact are from animal husbandry schemes.

TABLE 4.5: Assets with the Selected Beneficiaries: Intact or Non-Intact

Scheme	Intact	Non-Intact	Total
Dairying	41	7	48
Tangha-Ghora	—	1	1
Sheep	—	1	1
Pumpsets	9	—	9
Shop	1	—	1
	51 (85)	9 (15)	60 (100)

Note: Figures in parentheses are percentage of total.
Source: Author's field study.

The above analysis can be further supported by an evaluation report of IRDP conducted by the Government of Punjab in the year 1987 in three districts such as Hoshiarpur, Bhatinda and Sangrur. The results regarding the status of assets held by selected beneficiaries are shown in Table 4.6. The perusal of Table 4.6 shows that the assets of 82.50

per cent beneficiaries were found intact on the date of survey. It is also evident that about 15 per cent of the beneficiaries who adopted animal husbandry schemes had no animal or cart at the time of survey. Out of 45 cases in secondary sector activities, 11 cases (24%) were not intact. In the tertiary sector, 13 out of 57 beneficiaries who were given loans and subsidies opening a small business/shop were not having their assets intact with them.[11]

TABLE 4.6: Status of Assets held by Selected Beneficiaries

Scheme	Status of assets		Total
	In Position	Disappeared on the date or Survey	
1. Animal husbandry including bullock-cart mule/camel cart	213 (85.20)	37 (14.80)	250 (100)
2. Thresher	2	—	2
3. Secondary sector activities	34 (75.56)	11 (24.44)	45 (100)
4. Small business/shops	44 (77.19)	13 (22.81)	57 (100)
5. Sewing and knitting	4	2	6
Overall	297 (82.50)	63 (17.50)	360 (100)

Source: Government of Punjab, IRDP. An Evaluation, publication no. 544, The Economic Advisor of Government.

Impact on Income of the Beneficiaries

The success of the programme can be evaluated by working out the absolute increase in income and the beneficiaries crossing the poverty line. A small increase in the disposable income of the beneficiary can be a step towards the improvement in the quality of life of the family. Therefore, before we examine the impact of IRDP on the sample beneficiaries in terms of crossing the poverty line, we shall discuss the income generation effects of the programme in absolute sense. Our field study[12] shows that the income of the beneficiaries increased with the adoption of scheme sponsored under IRDP. The analysis shows that the different schemes adopted under the programme have increased the family income of landless labourers, marginal farmers and small farmers by about 26, 29 and 6 per cent, respectively.

There are certain surveys conducted in the Punjab which show a dismal picture of the IRDP. For example in an evaluation of IRDP by the Economic Adviser to the Punjab Government, it has been observed that only 33 per cent beneficiaries reported an upward shift in their income, whereas 62 per cent of the beneficiaries did not find any change in their income. It means that about 2/3 of the total beneficiaries were in the same condition in which they were before adopting the beneficiary scheme.

The Concurrent Evaluation Survey conducted for 22 States and union territories has shown that in Punjab 15 per cent of the beneficiaries experienced either a decline or no increase in family income after the adoption of IRDP asset. Rest of the 85 per cent of the beneficiaries reported an increase in their family income. It has been found that the 32 per cent of the beneficiaries experienced an increase in family income up to 50 per cent, an other 24 per cent between 51 and hundred per cent and 24 per cent had an increase of over 100 per cent. It points to the fact that 52 per cent of the sample beneficiaries who had experienced more than 50 per cent increase in the family income, irrespective of the value of assets given to them or the absolute increase in their income, can be considered to have gained significantly in terms of family welfare.

The above analysis shows that a seizable chunk of the assets of beneficiaries assisted under IRD programme has not generated income. In this connection, our earlier discussion may explain the reasons for this. It is possible that the assets generating zero income may not be intact with the beneficiary households. Other reasons may be defective asset, high maintenance cost of the asset, lack of infrastructure etc. It points to the fact that 'an IRDP asset might have changed the status of a beneficiary from a wage-earner to a self-employed without substantially changing the family income. It may be highly successful case of IRDP assistance in terms of the absolute income generated by the asset, but may not necessarily improve the net disposable income of the family.'[13] This explains the fact that it is not necessary that all the beneficiary households assisted under IRDP may have also crossed the poverty line.

Beneficiaries Crossing the Poverty Line

The crux of the IRD programme is to provide assistance to beneficiaries for purchasing productive assets so that it should add to the family income and help them in crossing the poverty line. Now the question arises whether the programme would be able to raise the assisted beneficiaries above the defined poverty line. Unless such a shift is achieved, the programme would be helping more and more poor people without mitigating their poverty. In Punjab, 3.96 Lakh beneficiary households were assisted under the various schemes of IRDP during the Sixth Plan period (1980-85). The number of families living below the poverty line in the rural areas as per Weaker Section Survey carried out in 1980-81 were 7.44 lakh and the number of additional families identified as poor after the survey up to 1985 were 2.17 lakh. Thus the total number of households identified as the below poverty line were 9.61 lakh up to 1985. If we assume that all the assisted beneficiaries under the programme during Sixth Plan had crossed the poverty line then 41 per cent of the total poor households would have crossed the poverty line during Sixth Five Year Plan. This depicts a good performance of the programme.

As stated above, it may not be necessary that all the assisted families under IRDP would have crossed the poverty line. The review of different studies pertaining to the Punjab will give us a rough and broad estimate about the beneficiaries who actually crossed the poverty line.

A comprehensive study[14] was conducted by the NABARD about the implementation of IRDP. The study concluded that there were wide variations of percentage of beneficiaries crossing the poverty line among the various States in India. It was found that the Punjab showed a better performance with more than 40 per cent of the poor families arising above the poverty line in the post-adoption of IRDP.

The Programme Evaluation Organisation (PEO)[15] study showed that by taking a cut-off point of an annual income of Rs. 3,500, only 169 out of 227 beneficiaries were real target families in agriculturally developed areas (which include Punjab, Haryana and costal areas of AP) in 1980-81 but 56.2 per cent beneficiaries of the total target families were able to cross the poverty line.

The author during his field study of three districts of Punjab found that out of 31 below poverty line households before the inclusion of scheme income, 19 households, i.e., 61 per cent had crossed the poverty line after the inclusion of scheme income.

The Concurrent Evaluation Survey found that the percentage of the eligible sample beneficiaries who had crossed the poverty line of Rs. 3,500 in 1985 were 85 per cent in Punjab. But when the minimum level of family income for the poverty line, which was fixed in 1979, was adjusted to inflation or revised according to the guidelines of the Seventh Five Year Plan, the percentage of eligible beneficiaries emerged out of poverty line due to the programme would certainly be small.

On the basis of above studies we assume, that atleast 40 to 50 per cent of the beneficiaries may have crossed the poverty line in Punjab. Let we assume that roughly 50 per cent of the families have crossed the poverty line. It means that out of 3.96 lakh assisted families under IRDP, approximately 1.98 lakh families, i.e., 50 per cent of the assisted families might have crossed the poverty line during 1980-85. It points to the fact that even if 1.98 lakh families had crossed the poverty line in Punjab during the Sixth Plan, there were 7.62 lakh families still below the poverty line up to 1985. This figure is more than what it was in 1980-81. It gives us the impression that the assistance under IRDP might have relatively reduced the families below poverty line but the programme has not made a significant dent in the reduction of absolute number of rural poor families in Punjab. This shows the inadequacy of the programme.

Repayment of Loans

One of the major criticism levelled against IRDP is relating to the poor performance of repayment of loans by the beneficiaries. In other words, the number of defaulters of the programme are increasing. The defaulters of the programme are those who are either irregular in repayment[16] or have stopped paying the loan instalment. It is a serious concern of the banks because the recycling of loans is necessary for effective working of the financial institutions. In the past, the co-operative credit institutions could not click because of the increasing number of defaulters and overdues. Therefore, the success of the programme depends upon the position of repayment of loans with the beneficiaries of IRDP. The bankers also feel if their investment is not properly recycled by the borrowers of the programme, it can cast its shadow on the industrial finance. Therefore, repayment of loan at proper time is very necessary and important. A number of studies have reported the weak repayment position of IRDP beneficiaries.

The study conducted by PEO of Planning Commission, New Delhi,[17] shows that there were 70 per cent of the overdues in respect of the repayment of the loans advanced in one of the two districts selected in Punjab. It means that in real terms no instalment had been repaid after adjustment of the subsidies. It is a serious concern of the financial institutions. The defaulters often complained against the inadequacy of returns from the scheme and poor marketing facilities and hence they were not in a position to make regular repayment.

In a survey,[18] the District Rural Development Agency of Patiala found that during Sixth Plan Period (1980-85) nearly 50 per cent of the loans were estimated to have been defaulted. The extent of default was 80 to 90 per cent in case of loans given for milch animals, poultry and piggery. Many of the beneficiaries were found to have sold the assets purchased with the help of loans.

The author during his field survey of three districts in Punjab e.g., Gurdaspur, Ludhiana and Faridkot found that 40 per cent of total beneficiaries either did not pay the loan instalment regularly or had stopped paying owing to the obvious reasons of fake purchases, poor quality of assets, lack of working capital etc. Most of the rural poor had been waiting for their loans up to Rs. 5,000 to have been written off by Akali (Barnala) Government as was promised to them during the election campaign in 1985. Milch animals were supplied to the beneficiaries without keeping in view the demand for milk in the villages and nearby towns. It was experienced that the plight of landless beneficiaries was miserable. They had not enough supply of cattle-feed, fodder and health care for their animals. They were not even in possession of a cattle-shed to house the animals in case of odd weather. It has also been observed that the extent of default was much higher in case of loans given for livestock, particularly milch animals than those of other schemes.

The results of the Concurrent Evaluation Survey conducted in 1985 indicate that 74 per cent of the beneficiaries started repayment of the loan up to three years. There were 61 per cent of the sample beneficiaries having no overdues and the overdues of another 39 per cent beneficiaries varied among different amounts. For example, the survey shows that 22 per cent of the beneficiaries had overdue amount up to Rs.1,000 and other beneficiaries had the overdue amount more than Rs.1,000. The main reasons for default were inadequate income, unforeseen calamity, tight repayment schedule etc. There is a need for indepth study of defaults by the beneficiaries of IRDP by the banks, research organisations and researchers. The investigation of these reasons can help the planners and the banks to frame suitable policies for greater realisation of loans.

The above analysis shows that there is a problem of realisation of borrowed money from the beneficiaries of IRDP. The steps must be taken to understand and removing the difficulties of the borrowers. The repayment position of loans must be improved for better performance of IRDP.

NOTES

1. (a) A.C. Kutty Krishnan in his study of a few villages of Kerala found only 20 per cent households below poverty line.
   A.C. Kutty Krishnan. 'A Case Study of IRDP in a Kerala village', *IJAE*, Vol. XXXIX, No.3, July-September, 1985.
   (b) The NABARD (1984) survey shows that percentage of beneficiaries misclassified to be 42 per cent in Assam, 18 per cent in Haryana, 35 per cent in Punjab, 19 per cent in M.P., 13 per cent in Maharashtra, 11 per cent in some of the districts of Tamil Nadu and Karnataka etc.
   NABARD (1984), Study of Implementation of IRDP (memo), Bombay.
   (c) Tripathy *et. al.* (1983) in their survey of SFDA/IRDP in Puri district of Orissa concluded that 13 per cent of the sample beneficiaries were clearly ineligible under the scheme. 'In a large number of cases persons do secure subsidy and bank credit although their known sources of income from farm and non-farm activities would make them totally ineligible for such assistance.'
   R.N. Tripathy *et. al.* (1983), 'Benefits to the Rural Poor: Process and problems of SFDA/IRDP: A study of Puri district', *Journal of Rural Development* Vol. II pp. 423 to 443.
2. NABARD (1984) *ibid.*
3. *Evaluation Study Report on IRDP for 1983-84*, The Programme Evaluation Organisation, Planning Commission, New Delhi.
4. R.K. Mahajan (1988), Differential Gains of IRDP in Punjab, project report sponsored by ICSSR, New Delhi.
5. N.J. Kurian, "IRDP: How Relevant is it?", *EPW*, December 26, 1987, pp. A-161 to A-187.
6. (a) It is mentioned in the PEO's study that 80 per cent of the beneficiaries adopted the schemes under primary sector.
   (b) Prof. Rath also found that the major type of asset creation for which loans (and subsidy) have been given is livestock, including dairy animals, goats, sheep as well as bullocks and bullockcarts.
   Nilkantha Rath, "Garibi Hatao — Can IRDP Do It?", *EPW*, February, 1985, pp. 238-246.
7. (a) An Evaluation study of IRDP conducted by the Punjab National Bank found that 60 per cent of the 97 beneficiaries were assisted for the purchase of one buffalo.
   Evaluation Cell, Management Advisory and Service Division, Punjab National Bank, New Delhi, 1984.

(b) Draft Seventh Five Year Plan (1985-90), Planning Commission, Government of India, accepted that the selection of schemes under the programme has shown an overwhelming bias towards animal husbandry, more particularly milch animals.

8. (a) Concurrent Evaluation Survey (1985-86) of IRDP, conducted by reputed research institutions sponsored by Department of Rural Development of Government of India during 1985-86, reveals the similar picture of Punjab. During the year under discussion, 64 per cent of the total beneficiaries adopted animal husbandry schemes, whereas only 10 per cent and 24 per cent of the total beneficiaries were assisted under secondary and tertiary sector schemes, respectively.

(b) An Evaluation of the IRDP by the PEO of the Planning Commission has brought out on the basis of informations collected from the selected beneficiaries of Ferozepur and Sangrur districts that 72 per cent and 80 per cent of the beneficiaries of these two districts, respectively, received assistance under primary sector activities. Within this sector, most of the selected beneficiaries were provided with animal husbandry units, mostly milch-cattle. About 2 to 3 per cent of the sample beneficiaries were provided with secondary sector schemes.
PEO, *op. cit.*

9. (a) In a study of Jaipur, Kanta Ahuja and Pardeep Bhargava reported that about 54 per cent of the beneficiaries assisted under IRDP had not asset with them. Either they had sold the asset or the animal was dead.
Kanta Ahuja and Pardeep Bhargava (1984), *IRDP : An Evaluation of Jaipur district*, Institute of Development Studies, Jaipur.

(b) The NABARD (1984) survey shows that about 26 per cent of leakages of loans for animal husbandry about half of it was due to misuse of loan and the other half was due to sale of aminals.
NABARD (1984) *op. cit.*

10. N.J. Kurian, *op. cit.* A-166.

11. The findings of Concurrent Evaluation Survey show that in Punjab only 68 per cent of the beneficiaries have the assets intact with them after two years of the assistance given under the programme. In the remaining 32 per cent cases the assets were either sold or fully perished or partly perished/defective or not even purchased.
Government of India, "Concurrent Evaluation of IRDP", February, 1987.

12. R.K. Mahajan, *op. cit.*

13. N.J. Kurien *op. cit.* p. A-170.

14. NABARD, *op. cit.*

15. Evaluation Study Report on IRDP for 1983-84, The Programme Evaluation Organisation, Planning Commission, New Delhi.

16. According to RBI guidelines, all IRDP loans should be medium term loans, that is, the repayment schedule should be atleast three years.

17. PEO (1985), *op. cit.*

18. The results of the survey were reported in *The Tribune* dated April 4, 1986.

FIVE

DIFFERENTIAL GAINS OF IRDP: A Micro Level Study

THE IRDP's target group consists of the poorest of the rural poor, small and marginal farmers, agricultural and non-agricultural labourers, scheduled castes and scheduled tribe families etc. who live below the poverty line. The main aim of the programme is to provide income generating assets and employment opportunities to the rural poor to enable them to raise above the poverty line. The IRDP in effect seeks to re-distribute assets and employment opportunities in favour of the rural poor. These aims can only be realised if the implementation of the programme is proper, i.e., the poorest of the poor families are taken first. The productive assets should be such that it generates sufficient income and employment to rise them above poverty line. Therefore, there is a need to seek answers for the specific questions. What are the types of assets given to the beneficiaries? What are the gains of IRDP to the beneficiaries in terms of income, assets, consumption in relation to non-beneficiaries? Is the increase in income sufficient to raise the beneficiaries above poverty line? What are inequalities in income, consumption and assets between beneficiaries and non-beneficiaries of IRDP, and owners of land and landless in the study area? This chapter, based upon the primary data, attempts to answer these questions.

Objectives of Study

The objective of the present study is to enquire into the gains of IRD programme in terms of income, consumption and employment to different beneficiary target groups and to compare them with non-beneficiaries. Obviously, it is difficult to explain as to why a number of beneficiaries of the programme have failed to cross the poverty line, in spite the availability of cheap credit and subsidised productive assets to them. The study also examines the problems and prospects of the programme. The specific objectives of the study are

(a) to assess the benefits of IRDP to different beneficiaries in terms of income, consumption and assets in relation to non-beneficiaries;
(b) to measure the inequalities in income, consumption and assets between beneficiaries and non-beneficiaries of IRDP, and owners and non-owners in the study area;
(c) to discuss the employment of beneficiaries and non-beneficiaries of the programme; and
(d) to examine the problems and prospects of the IRDP.

Material and Methods

The present study is conducted in Punjab where IRD programme was started in 1978. It was envisaged in the beginning that the programme would be implemented in a cluster of five contiguous villages in each of 117 blocks in the State. However, in 1980, the programme was given a new shape and was extended to all the 117 blocks of the State. The period of 9 years is sufficient for the programme to show its results. This is a study evaluating the gains of IRDP which highlights the success and failure of the programme.

A study of evaluation of a programme can be conducted on the basis of time series data or cross-section data. In this study, the main tool of investigation is cross-section of respondents. Therefore, the beneficiaries and non-beneficiaries of the programme are examined carefully for evaluating the impact of the programme.

The data required for this study are collected from field survey and secondary sources keeping in view the objectives of the study.

Study Area

This study is confined to three districts of Punjab. The districts are selected in such a way that different parts of the State get representation in the study. Punjab is divided into three broad homogeneous zones, on agroclimatic and soil type basis. The details are given below:

Zone I

This is the Kandi zone of the State. It comprises of the north-western sides of the State. It consists of Gurdaspur, Hoshiarpur and Ropar districts.

Zone II

The central zone of the State comprises of the districts Amritsar, Jalandhar, Kapurthala, Ludhiana and Patiala, Moga tahsil of Faridkot and Malerkotla tahsil of Sangrur.

Zone III

The south-western zone of the state includes the districts of Ferozepur and Bhatinda, Faridkot and Muktsar tahsils of district Faridkot, and Barnala, Sunam and Sangrur tahsils of Sangrur district.

The main aim of dividing the State into three zones is to compare the impact of the programme zone to zone.

From each zone, one district was selected purposely viz. Gurdaspur from the first zone, Ludhiana from second and Faridkot from the third zone. Only those districts were included for the purpose of study where IRD programme was working well.

Selection of Blocks and Villages

It was proposed to select three blocks, one each from a district. The selection of blocks was made in consultation with the officials of District Rural Development Agencies.

For the selection of the villages, a list of those villages was prepared from the block office where the IRD programme had been working successfully. Out of this list, two villages were selected on random basis. In this way, six villages were selected for the purpose of the study. The districts, blocks and villages selected are given in Table 5.1.

However, the results presented in this study are based on only five villages. Despite the best efforts of the investigator, the survey in one of the villages of Batala block, Chahal, could not be carried out due to the incidents of violence and frequent curfew at the block headquarters. Therefore, in order to present the results in time, the investigator had to leave the idea of surveying the village.

TABLE 5.1: Selection of Districts, Blocks and Villages

Name of district	Name of block	Name of villages
1. Gurdaspur	1. Batala	1. Nathwal 2. Chahal
2. Ludhiana	2. Sudhar	1. Sudhar 2. Akalgarh
3. Faridkot	3. Malout	1. Jandwala 2. Khane-Di-Dhab
3	3	6

Selection of Respondents

For the selection of respondents, a list of all yellow-card holders[1] (target families) was prepared. This group comprises of mainly marginal and small farmers, landless labourers, scheduled castes and petty shop-keepers. The yellow-card holders were further divided into two categories, beneficiary and non-beneficiary households. From each village, samples of 12 beneficiary and equal number of non-beneficiary households were selected by using random sampling technique. In order to give equal representation to landless and landowner families, three marginal farmers, three small farmers and six landless labourers were selected at random. On all 120 households were surveyed, 60 beneficiary and 60 non-beneficiary households, for the purpose of the present study. The sample scheme is presented in Table 5.2.

TABLE 5.2: Sample Scheme

Category	Blocks							
	Batala		Sudhar		Malout		Total	
	B	NB	B	NB	B	NB	B	NB
Marginal	3	3	6	6	6	6	15	15
Small	3	3	6	6	6	6	15	15
Landless	6	6	12	12	12	12	30	30
Total	12	12	24	24	24	24	60	60

B = Beneficiary NB = Non-Beneficiary

Data Collection

Primary data were collected with the help of a schedule especially designed for this study. The information from respondents was collected by coming directly face-to-face with them. Before canvassing the schedule to the respondents, it was pre-tested and necessary corrections were made in it. The schedule was designed in such a manner as to reflect the socio-economic characteristics, pattern of income, consumption, capital formation, employment, assets etc. of beneficiary and non-beneficiary households.

In addition to the primary data, the study was enriched by using the data from secondary sources. Secondary data were collected from Block Development Office, District Rural Development Agency (DRDA), Rural Development and Panchayat Department of Punjab, Ministry of Rural Development, New Delhi, Statistical Digest of Punjab, Journals and published and unpublished reports.

This study took sample from those beneficiaries who were benefited under IRD programme from 1983 to 1985 in the selected study area. The year of assessment was 1985-86.

Data Analysis

After scrutiny of the collected data from the field it was processed according to the objectives laid down for the study. In general, simple tabular analysis was carried out based on averages, frequency distribution and percentages.

In order to assess the income and asset distribution pattern of the target groups with and without scheme under IRDP, the following methods are used:

Lorenz Curve and the Gini Concentration Ratio

The Lorenz Curve is a graphic method of studying the dispersion in a distribution. This curve is drawn by plotting cumulative values of the variable and the cumulative frequency when the units are arranged in an ascending or descending order. The diagonal line is called the line of perfect equality. The farther the curve from the line of perfect equality, the more will be the income inequalities and *vice versa*. An obvious weakness of the Lorenz Curve is that it does not give the numerical value of the variability for the given distribution. Therefore, this measure must be supplemented with some numerical measure.

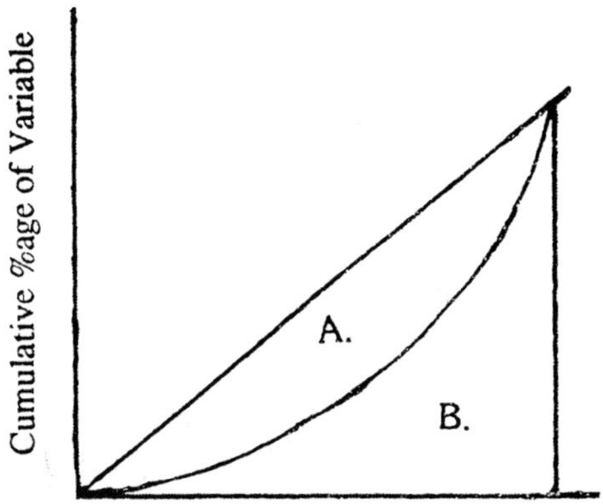

Cumulative %age of H.H.

Gini-ratio measure the degree of inequality. This ratio can be approximated from the Lorenz Curve. It represents the proportion of the area under the diagonal that lies between diagonal and the Lorenz Curve. If the area inside the Lorenz Curve is assumed as 'A' and outside the Lorenz Curve as'B' the ratio would be

$$A/(A+B)$$

If there were perfect equality, the ratio of concentration would be zero. This ratio would be 1 if there were perfect inequality. Hence, the range of this ratio is from zero to one.

The Standard Deviation of the Logarithms of the Income and Assets

This is a popular measure. It is defined as

$$SD = \left[\frac{1}{N} \sum_{i=1}^{N} (\log x_i - \log \overline{x})^2 \right]^{1/2}$$

where N is the total number of individuals and X_i is the income/asset of each individual or household.

Such as Gini-ratio, this measure is also invariant with respect to proportional shifts in all incomes/assets and is sensitive to disproportionate changes at all levels of income/asset. But it attaches more weight tó transfers at the lower end of the distribution.[2]

The Coefficient of Variation

It is defined as

$$CV = \left[\frac{1}{N} \sum_{i=1}^{N} (x_i - \overline{x})^2 \right]^{1/2}$$

In the above formula
N = total number of households.
X_i = Family income of each household.

This measure, such as Gini-ratio and standard deviation of the logarithms of the incomes, is also unaffected by equal proportional increases in all incomes and is sensitive to disproportionate changes at all levels of income.

The concept of employment is used as the total human labour utilises on the farm and other operations. Female and child labour is converted into adult mandays as follows:

1 female labour day = 3/4 adult male-day,
1 child labour day = 1/2 adult male-day.

Where the wages of male and female labour are same, the above adjustment is not followed.

Concepts and Variables Used

Here, the meaning and methods of measuring the variables and concepts used in the study are presented.

Beneficiary and Non-Beneficiary Households

Beneficiary households are those who have adopted any of the income generating schemes assisted under IRD programme after 1983, but before 1985.

Non-beneficiary includes all those households which belong to target group but they have not been benefited from the programme.

Target Group

The terms 'target group' and 'weaker sections' have been

interchangeably used. The target group comprises of landless agricultural/non-agricultural labourers, tenants and rural artisans, small and marginal farmers, scheduled castes etc. These target group households are provided with yellow-cards by the Government of Punjab, on the basis of a State-wide survey undertaken in September 1980. All those households earning less than Rs. 3,600 per annum in the survey year[3] were given yellow cards to enable them to take advantage of the facilities available to the poor.

Marginal and Small Farmers

Marginal farmer is a farmer who operates on land less than 2.5 acres. Small farmer operates on land between 2.5 acres and 5 acres. Though different zones in Punjab were selected for the purpose of study, no effort has been made to standardise the land of different regions.

Agricultural/Non-Agricultural Labour

Agricultural/non-agricultural labourer is a landless person who receives more than 50 per cent of his income for agricultural/non-agricultural wages.

Income

It is very crucial concept for the purpose of study. It includes the following types of income:

Income through Crop Enterprise: This type of income is computed by taking the difference of the value of farm output (main + by-product) and costs of production. The cost concepts used in the study were taken from 'Farm Management Studies'. Accordingly the following concepts of income are used.

(i) *Net Income*: This is the difference between the value of gross output and total expenditure e.g., gross output minus cost C.

(ii) *Family Labour Income*: It includes net income plus the imputed wages for the labour of farmer and his family. Thus, it is the gross income minus cost B.

(iii) *Farm Business Income (FBI)*: It is obtained by adding up the family labour income, the unpaid interest on owned capital and unpaid rent on owned land. Thus, it is gross income minus cost

A_2.

For the purpose of income of the agricultural household, the concept of farm Business Income is used.

Income from Livestock (LI): This source of income includes returns from family and labour management from livestock e.g., dairying, poultry, sheep rearing etc.

Scheme Income(SI): This concept is applicable to the beneficiary households only. The efforts are made to calculate the addition in income due to adoption of income generating scheme under IRD programme.

Wage Income(WI): This includes income accrued to the labourers from hiring out labour for agricultural operations or/and non-agricultural jobs. Therefore, wages can be agricultural or/and non-agricultural.

Income From Other Sources (OI): This includes income from other than above mentioned sources.

Hypothesis

The following hypotheses are proposed for the study:

H_1

Weaker sections of the society get the procedural difficulties in getting the project and loan sanctioned from DRDA and financial agencies.

H_2

(a) IRDP has increased per family and per capita income and consumption of beneficiaries of the programme compared to non-beneficiaries. Since, the programme provides productive asset to the beneficiary household, this helps in the reduction of poverty among the weaker sections.

(b) The benefits of the programme are unevenly spread between landless beneficiaries and land owner beneficiaries.

H_3

IRDP has made possible for the beneficiary household to adopt non-farm activities such as dairying, poultry etc. to increase their family income compared to non-beneficary households.

H_4

The additional employment provided under IRDP for the landless and marginal farmers under non-farm activities is not sufficient.

Limitations of the Study

(1) The economic condition of both beneficiaries and non-beneficiaries was supposed to be almost same before the adoption of income generating scheme under IRDP in the study area.

(2) This is a cross-sectional study, therefore, at the most it compares the economic disparities of beneficiaries and non-beneficiaries at a point of time.

(3) Due to time and resource constraint, data are collected from a few villages of Punjab and results may be reflected for Punjab as a whole.

(4) This study does not cover exclusively salaried class.

The Results

The 60 beneficiary households selected from five villages of three blocks of Punjab contain a total population of 395 persons comprising 215 males and 181 females. The 60 non-beneficiary households represent population of 365 persons comprising of 206 males and 159 females.

About 54 per cent of the total beneficiaries are in the age group of 15-59 years, whereas this proportion is 60 per cent in case of non-beneficiaries. These results are almost similar to census of Punjab, 1981. About 41 per cent of beneficiaries and 33 per cent of non-beneficiaries belong to category of children, i.e., in the age group of 14 years or less.

Social Status

The social classification of the selected beneficiary and non-beneficiary households shows that 80 per cent of beneficiary and

93 per cent non-beneficiary landless households belong to scheduled castes. But landowner beneficiary and non-beneficiary households are mostly from higher castes. Only 17 per cent of the beneficiary and 20 per cent of the non-beneficiary landowner households belong to scheduled castes and backward classes. The overall analysis shows that 52 per cent of the beneficiary and 57 per cent of the non-beneficiary households belong to scheduled and backward castes.

Size of Holding

Size of holding is an important variable which affects the income, consumption, saving and investment of landowner households. Table 5.3 shows the average size of the farms of marginal and small farmers.

TABLE 5.3: Distribution of Selected Farms and Area according to Type and Size

(Acres)

Size	No. of Farmers	Total operation area			Percent-age to total	Average farm size
		Irrigated	Unirriga-ted	Total		
Beneficiary						
Marginal	15	26.75	1.0	27.75	30.92	1.850
Small	15	62.00	—	62.00	69.08	4.133
Overall	30	88.75	1.0	89.75	100.00	2.992
Non-Beneficiary						
Marginal	15	25.38	—	25.38	31.38	1.692
Small	15	52.50	3.0	55.50	67.62	3.700
Overall	30	77.88	3.0	80.88	100.00	2.696

It will be observed from Table 5.3 that average farm size of marginal and small beneficiary farmers is larger than that of the non-beneficiary farmers of the same categories. Overall average size of holding of beneficiaries is 2.99 acres whereas it is 2.70 acres in case of non-beneficiaries. The average farm size of the beneficiary marginal farmers is 1.85 acres whereas it is 1.69 acres for the non-beneficiary counterparts.

Benefit Schemes

Under IRD programme, a beneficiary is free to opt for any viable economic activity which enables him to cross poverty line. The scheme should be covered under any one of the three sectors : primary, secondary and tertiary. Most of the benefit schemes adopted by the beneficiaries in Punjab belong to either primary or tertiary sectors. Information collected from all the selected beneficiary households regarding the details of benefit schemes in the study area are presented in Table 5.4

TABLE 5.4: Distribution of Sample Households by Benefit Schemes Financed under IRDP

Category	Number of households provided assistance under IRDP schemes				
	Animal husbandry schemes	Petty grocery shop	Mechanical inputs	Others	Total
Landless	27 (90.00)	1 (3.33)	—	2 (6.67)	30 (100)
Marginal Farmers	15 (100.00)	—	—	—	15 (100)
Small Farmers	6 (40.00)	—	9 (60.00)	—	15 (100)
Total	48	1	9	2	60

Note: Figures in parentheses are percentages.

The persual of Table 5.4 shows that animal husbandry schemes, particularly milch cattle are very popular with the selected beneficiaries. About 80 per cent of the total number of beneficiary households were benefited through milch-cattle. It seems that IRDP is a programme of dairy development in Punjab. Of the remaining 20 per cent households, 15 per cent households get assistance for tube-wells and 5 per cent for tertiary sector viz. shopkeeping, *tonga* and *ghora* (horse) etc. It is interesting to note that all the 15 beneficiary marginal farmers are benefited through milch-cattle whereas the small farmers install tube-wells to increase productivity of agriculture.

It is observed that the submission of application for the scheme to DRDA and the grant of sanction for loan to purchase the assets takes a lot of time.

The survey shows that only 25 per cent of the sample beneficiaries could get all the formalities settled within 3 months from the date of application. Another 52 per cent beneficiary households received the loan and asset between 3 to 9 months. Rest of the 23 per cent beneficiaries have to wait for more than nine months.

Landless labourers have to wait for longer period than land-owners. Thirty-three per cent of the landless labourers have to wait for more than 9 months to get finance for grounding the scheme.

Loan Amount Received

It is observed that majority of the beneficiaries (85%) received financial assistance up to Rs. 5,000. Remaining 15 per cent of the beneficiary households are in receipt of loans more than Rs. 5,000. All the beneficiary landless households get assistant up to Rs. 5,000. Most of the small farmers (53%) has managed to get assistance more than Rs. 5,000.

Repayment of Loan

It is observed that 60 per cent of the sample beneficiaries are paying loan instalments regularly till the time of survey and only 40 per cent are defaulters. The assets with most of the defaulters are missing. Some of the defaulters complain that the income generated by the assets is not sufficient to repay the loan instalment. A few of the defaulters reveal that they stop the repayment of the loan because Akalis promised to erase all the loans up to Rs. 5,000 during their election campaign. Thus about forty four per cent of the landless households and 25 per cent of the marginal farmers are found to be defaulters.

The repayment position of the beneficiary households is also poor. It is observed that 8.33 per cent of the beneficiaries have not repaid even a single instalment till the time of completion of the fieldwork. About 37 per cent of the beneficiaries repay only 20 per cent of the loan. A majority of the households of beneficiaries have repaid only between 20 to 50 per cent of the total amount of loan. It is also observed that landless households are more sluggish in repayment than that of marginal and small farmers.

Now we shall evaluate the gains of IRD programme on different categories of beneficiaries and the details have been worked out in terms of income, consumption, assets and employment of labour. A comparative study of these variables between beneficiary and non-beneficiary households is also undertaken. This study is divided into four sections. Section I deals with income of beneficiaries and non-beneficiaries and the extent of income inequalities. Section II discusses the pattern of consumption of different categories of households. The composition of assets and its distribution is discussed in section III. Section IV analyses the employment of labour.

I. INCOME AND ITS DISTRIBUTION

An attempt is made in this section to discuss income generating capacity of the scheme adopted under IRD programme by the beneficiaries. The income generation is estimated by taking with and without scheme-income at the same point of time. The main aim of the analysis is to estimate the precise income impact of the programme. The income difference between beneficiaries and non-beneficiaries has also been studied.

Further, the concentration of income among beneficiaries and non-beneficiaries and landowners and landless is discussed in this section. The main tools of analysis for measurement of inequality are Lorenz Curve and Gini Coefficient Ratio (GCR).

The study takes into account the concept of family income and per capita income. For the purpose of calculation of family income, the following methodology is adopted.

The following abbreviations are used:*

(1) Family Business Income from Agriculture	= FBI
(2) Income from Wages (Agricultural and Non-Agricultural)	= WI
(3) Income from Other Sources	= OI
(4) Income from Livestock	= LI
(5) Scheme Income	= SI
(6) Family Income	= FI

On the basis of the above abbreviations, the following concepts of income are used:

$$FI(NB)_C^{*} = FBI + WI + LI + OI$$

$$FI(NB)_L^{**} = WI + LI + OI$$

* = $(NB)_C$ = Non-Beneficiary Cultivator.
= $(NB)_L$ = Non-Beneficiary Landless.
= $(B)_C$ = Beneficiary Cultivators.
= $(B)_L$ = Beneficiary Landless.

$$FI(B)_C^{@} = FBI + WI + LI + OI + SI$$

$$FI(B)_C^{S} = WI + LI + OI + SI$$

Pattern and Source of Income of Beneficiaries and Non-Beneficiaries

Table 5.5 presents the different sources of income to the sample households of different blocks in Punjab. The major sources of income of the sample beneficiaries are agriculture, agricultural wages, other wages, IRDP scheme income and income from other sources. Non-beneficiary households include all the sources of income except IRDP scheme-income.

The perusal of Table 5.5 shows that the average income of beneficiaries both landowners and landless is higher than their non-beneficiary counterparts. Family income per household of landless beneficiary is Rs. 7,863 as compared to Rs. 5,332 of the non-beneficiary of the same category. The income of the landowners (marginal + small farmers) beneficiary is higher (Rs. 10,383) than non-beneficiary (Rs. 8,465). As expected, the income of the landless sample household is accrued from wages, both agricultural and non-agricultural. It is interesting to note that landowner beneficiary households receive about 87 per cent of the income from agriculture and 12 per cent from the adoption of the IRDP scheme, whereas the non-beneficiaries get 94 per cent of their total income from agriculture only. It points to the fact that the income of the landowner beneficiaries is diversified, whereas the income of the non-beneficiaries is dependent on a single source. The 79 per cent of the income of the landless beneficiary accrues from wages and 21 per cent from the scheme sponsored by IRDP, whereas 98 per cent of the income of the landless non-beneficiaries is from wages only.

It is evident from the above discussion that the income of the beneficiaries is high and diversified as compared with the income of the non-beneficiaries. The income derived from IRDP scheme by the beneficiaries is estimated to be 21 per cent for landless, 20 per cent for marginal farmers and 8 per cent for small farmers. It is interesting to note that with the adoption of IRDP, the relative importance of agriculture, agricultural wages and other wages have decreased in the family income per beneficiary household.

TABLE 5.5: Family Income Per Household by Source and Block

(Rs.)

Source of Income	Malout (Faridkot)		Sudhar (Ludhiana)		Batala (Gurdaspur)		Overall (Punjab)	
	B	NB	B	NB	B	NB	B	NB
1	2	3	4	5	6	7	8	9
Agricultural Income								
Landless	—	—	—	—	—	—	—	—
Landowner	6187 (85.35)	6279 (93.79)	11553 (88.87)	9916 (94.68)	9924 (84.00)	7208 (92.13)	9081 (87.46)	7919 (93.55)
Marginal	3642 (74.21)	4382 (91.33)	6689 (81.47)	5849 (93.34)	3947 (60.84)	2125 (71.84)	4922 (77.09)	4517 (90.65)
Small	8732 (91.06)	8175 (95.15)	16417 (92.28)	13981 (95.21)	15901 (92.77)	12291 (96.85)	13240 (92.07)	11321 (95.02)
Agricultural Wages								
Landless	5728 (64.42)	5124 (83.67)	4720 (66.65)	4354 (84.33)	3452 (53.34)	3567 (87.34)	4870 (61.94)	4505 (84.49)
Landowner	—	125 (1.87)	200 (1.54)	558 (5.33)	—	616 (7.87)	80 (0.77)	396 (4.67)
Marginal	—	83 (1.73)	300 (3.65)	416 (6.64)	—	833 (28.16)	120 (1.88)	333 (6.67)
Small	—	167 (1.94)	100 (0.62)	700 (4.77)	—	400 (3.15)	40 (0.28)	426 (3.57)

Contd.

TABLE 5.5 *Contd.*

1	2	3	4	5	6	7	8	9
Other Wages								
Landless	1600	1000	1383	683	867	167	1367	707
	(17.19)	(16.33)	(18.36)	(13.23)	(13.41)	(4.09)	(17.38)	(13.26)
Landowner	—	—	—	—	—	—	—	—
Marginal	—	—	—	—	—	—	—	—
Small	—	—	—	—	—	—	—	—
IRDP Scheme Income								
Landless	1538	—	1430	—	2230	—	1616	—
	(17.31)		(18.98)		(34.49)		(20.55)	
Landowner	995	—	1247	—	1890	—	1195	—
	(13.73)		(9.59)		(16.00)		(11.51)	
Marginal	1133	—	1221	—	2540	—	1290	—
	(23.03)		(14.87)		(39.15)		(20.20)	
Small	857	—	1273	—	1240	—	1100	—
	(8.94)		(7.16)		(7.23)		(7.65)	
Other Sources								
Landless	25	—	—	125	—	350	10	120
	(0.28)			(2.42)		(8.57)	(0.13)	(2.25)

Landowner	67	375	—	—	—	—	27	150
	(0.92)	(5.60)					(0.26)	(1.77)
Marginal	133	333	—	—	—	—	53	133
	(2.71)	(6.94)					(0.83)	(2.67)
Small	—	416	—	—	—	—	—	167
		(4.84)						(1.40)
All Sources								
Landless	8891	6124	7534	5163	6466	4084	7863	5332
	(100)	(100)	(100)	(100)	(100)	(100)	(100)	(100)
Landowner	7249	6695	13000	10473	11814	7824	10383	8465
	(100)	(100)	(100)	(100)	(100)	(100)	(100)	(100)
Marginal	4908	4798	8210	6266	6487	2958	6385	4983
	(100)	(100)	(100)	(100)	(100)	(100)	(100)	(100)
Small	9589	8592	17790	14684	17141	12691	14380	11914
	(100)	(100)	(100)	(100)	(100)	(100)	(100)	(100)

Note: Figures in parentheses are percentages to total.
B = Beneficiary.
NB = Non-Beneficiary.

The average income from agricultural wages of landless is higher in Malout block (Rs. 5,728 for per beneficiary household and Rs. 5,124 for non-beneficiary) than that of Sudhar block of Ludhiana district (Rs. 4,720 and Rs. 4,354) and Batala block of Gurdaspur district (Rs. 3,452 and Rs. 3,567). It may be mainly due to the fact that cotton is the main crop of Malout block which requires a lot of labour, particularly for the picking up of cotton. Therefore, the landless labourers are engaged for more time than their counterparts in other blocks. On the other hand, the sample beneficiary and non-beneficiary cultivators of Sudhar block represent higher income than those of Batala and Malout blocks.

Income Variation Among Beneficiaries and Non-Beneficiaries

The Integrated Rural Development Programme directly attacks poverty by financing the income generating asset for the target households. The beneficiaries, therefore, can certainly improve their lot with the help of this programme. Despite a number of non-effective beneficiaries,[4] the upward increase in the income of beneficiaries is estimated.

The perusal of Table 5.5 shows that the landless labourers have larger differences in their income in all the selected blocks than marginal and small farmers. The average income of overall beneficiaries and non-beneficiaries is the highest in Sudhar block, i.e., Rs. 10,215 and Rs. 7,818 respectively. The difference of income between beneficiaries and non-beneficiaries is the largest in Batala block, i.e., 53.04 per cent. This difference is mainly due to the successful adoption of IRD programme in the beneficiary households. It is estimated that beneficiary landless and marginal farmers noticed a larger improvement in their income than small farmers. It may be due to the nature of income generating scheme. Most of the small farmers own tube-wells which generate benefits slowly. Secondly, there is no big difference between agricultural income per acre of beneficiary and non-beneficiary small farmers.

Income Range-wise Beneficiaries and Non-Beneficiaries

Before analysing the income distribution of different categories of households, it is important to look into the number of beneficiaries and non-beneficiaries according to different income ranges. It will help in studying the concentration of households in the various income groups and the number of families below poverty line at the time of survey.

Table 5.6 shows the sample beneficiaries according to various income ranges with and without scheme income. It is evident from the Table 5.6 that most of the beneficiaries belong to the income range of Rs. 4,800 to Rs. 7,500 in all the selected blocks. The second income range (without scheme income) where larger number of families concentrate is Rs. 3,500 to Rs. 4,800. The second largest concentration of beneficiaries (with scheme income) falls in income range Rs. 7,500 to Rs. 10,500.

It is also evident from Table 5.6 that in case of total beneficiaries, the first two income ranges; both falling below poverty line income; have experienced a decline in number of beneficiaries with scheme income as compared to without scheme-income. The percentage decline in the income ranges of below Rs.3,500 and Rs.3,500 to Rs.4,800 is 75 per cent and 80 per cent, respectively. In terms of absolute number 15 beneficiaries have shifted to higher income ranges as a result of scheme income.

The analysis of non-beneficiaries' income is presented in Table 5.7. The concentration of income of the non-beneficiaries is limited to the income group of Rs.4,800 to Rs.7,500. The perusal of Table 5.7 shows that about 50 per cent households of Malout and Sudhar blocks fall in this income range. The number of families below poverty line are 25 per cent in Malout, 21 per cent in Sudhar and 75 per cent in Batala block. Only 25 per cent of the total non-beneficiary households are having income over Rs.7500 per annum. It may be noted that a large number of non-beneficiaries do not fall under the category of target households. Theses households should not be assisted under IRDP because they do not deserve the benefit of subsidy.

Target Households

The main objective of IRD programme is to raise the target households above poverty line. For the analysis of this study, target family is with an annual family income of below Rs.4,800 or per capita income below Rs.960. In the absence of time series data of the sample households, the family income without scheme income is taken as the base for the purpose of estimating target households. The perusal of Table 5.6 shows that out of 60 households, only 19, i.e., 32 per cent, are below poverty line.[5] It is also observed that annual income of about 33 per cent of the households is above Rs.7,500. It points to the fact that 33 per cent of the beneficiaries belong to better-off sections.

TABLE 5.6: Different Income Groupwise Number of Beneficiary Households

District/Block	Beneficiary Households		Income Groups					
			Below Rs.3500	Rs.3500-Rs.4800	Rs.4800-Rs.7500	Rs.7500-Rs.10500	Rs.10500-Rs.15000	Rs.15000 & Above
Faridkot								
Malout	24(100)	A	2(8.33)	7(29.17)	8(33.33)	3(12.50)	4(16.67)	—
		B	1(4.16)	3(12.50)	9(37.50)	5(20.83)	5(20.83)	1(4.16)
Ludhiana								
Sudhar	24(100)	A	—	4(16.67)	10(41.66)	3(12.50)	4(16.67)	3(12.50)
		B	—	—	9(37.50)	6(25.00)	4(16.67)	5(20.83)
Gurdaspur								
Batala	12(100)	A	2(16.67)	4(33.33)	3(25.00)	—	1(8.33)	2(16.67)
		B	—	—	8(66.67)		1(8.33)	2(16.67)
Total	60(100)	A	4(6.67)	15(25.00)	21(35.00)	6(10.00)	9(15.00)	5(8.33)
		B	1(1.67)	3(5.00)	26(43.33)	12(20.00)	10(16.67)	8(13.33)
		C	-75.0	-80.0	23.8	100.0	11.11	60.0

Note: Figures in parentheses are percentages of total.
A = Without Scheme Income; B = With Scheme Income; C = Percentage Variation.

TABLE 5.7: Different Income Groupwise Number of Non-Beneficiary Households

District/ Block	Non-Beneficiary Households	Income Groups					
		Below Rs.3,500	Rs.3,500 Rs.4,800	Rs.4,800 Rs.7,500	Rs.7,500 Rs.10,500	Rs.10,500 Rs.15,000	Rs.15,000 Above
Faridkot							
Malout	24 (100)	1 (4.17)	5 (20.83)	13 (54.17)	2 (8.33)	3 (12.50)	—
Ludhiana							
Sudhar	24 (100)	1 (4.17)	4 (16.66)	12 (50.00)	1 (4.17)	4 (16.67)	2 (8.33)
Gurdaspur							
Batala	12 (100)	2 (16.67)	7 (58.33)	—	—	2 (16.67)	1 (8.33)
Total	60 (100)	4 (6.67)	16 (26.67)	25 (41.67)	3 (5.00)	9 (15.00)	3 (5.00)

Note: Figures in parentheses are percentages of total

The IRDP has raised the actual target families above poverty line by way of income generating assets. For example, the number of target households decreased from 32 per cent to 7 per cent with the inclusion of scheme income.

The above analysis takes into consideration the family income. Since the family-size differs significantly, it is worthwhile to examine the above results in terms of per capita annual income (PCI). The annual PCI of Rs.960 is taken as cut-off income of below poverty line. The household having this much or less income is treated as below poverty line. It can be noted from Table 5.8 that the proportion of below poverty line households on the basis of PCI is estimated to be 51.67 per cent.[6] Table 5.7 also shows that for 31.67 per cent of the households the per capita income lies between Rs.960-1,800 and for 16.67 per cent above Rs.1800. It is clear from the analysis that the programme has benefited about 48 per cent households which were already above poverty line. The scheme income, thus, appears to have provided relief to 32 per cent below poverty line per capita income households.

Shift of Beneficiaries to Higher Income Categories

An attempt is made here to assess the movement of beneficiaries in the income ladder after adoption of IRD programme. Table 5.8 shows the frequency distribution of beneficiaries of different categories – landless, marginal and small farmers. The shift of beneficiaries from lower to higher income group without and with the IRDP scheme for each category is presented in the Table 5.8.

TABLE 5.8: Shift of IRDP Beneficiaries from Lower to Higher Income Groups

Per capita Income range (Rs.)	Households			
	Landless	Marginal farmers	Small farmers	Overall
Below 750	A8(26.7)	6(40.0)	2(13.3)	16(26.7)
	B1(3.3)	3(20.0)	2(13.3)	6(10.0)
	C 87.5	-50.0	—	-62.5
750-960	A10(33.3)	5(33.3)	—	15(25.0)
	B4(13.3)	2(13.3)	—	6(10.0)
	C 60.0	-60.0	—	-60.0
960-1200	A6(20.0)	2(13.3)	1(6.7)	9(15.0)
	B15(50.0)	4(26.7)	—	19(31.7)
	C150.0	100.0	-100.0	111.11
1200-1800	A5(16.7)	2(13.3)	3(20.0)	10(16.7)
	B9(30.0)	6(40.0)	2(13.3)	17(28.3)
	C 80.0	200.0	33.3	70.0
1800-2500	A1(3.3)	--	2(13.3)	3(25.0)
	B --		3(20.0)	3(5.0)
	C 100.0	--	50.0	--
2500 & Above	A --		7(46.7)	7(11.7)
	B1(3.3)	--	8(53.3)	9(15.0)
	C --	14.38	28.6	
Total	30	15	15	60

Note: Figures in parentheses are percentages to total.
A = Without Scheme Income; B = With Scheme Income; C = Per cent Variation.

It is evident from Table 5.8 that the first two lower income groups, such as below Rs.750 and Rs.750-960, have experienced a decline in the number of beneficiaries after adoption of the scheme. Both these categories represent the households below poverty line. The decline in their number from this category due to adoption of income generating schemes under IRD programme is a good sign. Higher income categories are showing positive percentage variation. In absolute sense out of 31 households which were below poverty line before inclusion of the scheme income, 19 households have crossed the poverty line, i.e., 32 per cent crossed the poverty line.[7] There has been a greater shift in income of landless households than marginal farmers. The small farmers have already high income.

Table 5.9 is a summary Table showing number of beneficiary households crossing poverty line. It is clear from Table 5.9 that out of 60 families of beneficiary households 48 (80%) have crossed the poverty line with scheme under IRD programme. It is because their per capita income has increased beyond Rs.960. However, 29 families (44.33%) are already above poverty line without scheme income. Their inclusion may be due to wrong selection of the target households. Since this study takes income at a point of time, it may also be possible that some of the beneficiary households may be below poverty line when the scheme is financed to them. It is calculated that the net percentage of beneficiaries crossing poverty line at the time of survey is only 31.67 per cent for the State as a whole.

It is observed that IRD programme is helping landless households of Sudhar block in a big way. It is estimated that without scheme-income there were 16.67 per cent landless households above poverty line and their percentage increased to 83.33 after the adoption of the scheme. Thus the net per cent increase is 66.66. It is evident that no small farmer in Sudhar and Batala block is below poverty line. It shows that the small farmers are progressive and have comparatively high income.

Concentration of Income

There are a few accepted methods of studying income disparities. These methods are:

(i) Lorenz Curve,
(ii) Gini Coefficient Ratio,
(iii) Standard Deviation of Logarithms of Incomes; and
(iv) Coefficient of Variation.

The Lorenz Curve associated with a distribution gives a joint cumulation both of frequencies and of the variables being distributed in percentages. It is graphical representation of disparity in income distribution. Gini concentration ratio or Gini ratio is the ratio of the area that lies between the egalitarian line and the Lorenz Curve to the area that lies under the egalitarian line. The range of its value is from 0 to 1. Both, Lorenz Curve and Gini Ratio are not exclusive methods of measurement but are complementary to each other. The income distribution of beneficiary and non-beneficiary households has been measured by making use of these two methods.

TABLE 5.9: Summary Table showing Beneficiaries Crossing Poverty Line on the Basis of Per Capita Income

District/ Block		Without scheme income (Already above poverty line)		With scheme income (Above poverty line)		Net number crossing poverty line	
		No. of H.H.	Percentage	No. of H.H.	Percentage	No. of H.H.	Percentage
Faridkot	LL	8	66.67	11	91.67	3	25.00
Malout	M	1	16.67	3	50.00	2	33.33
	S	4	66.67	4	66.67	—	—
Total		13	54.17	18	75.00	5	20.83
Ludhiana							
Sudhar	LL	2	16.67	10	83.33	8	66.66
	M	3	50.00	5	83.33	2	33.33
	S	6	100.00	6	100.00	—	—
Total		11	45.83	21	87.50	10	41.67
Gurdaspur							
Batala	LL	2	33.33	4	66.66	2	33.33
	M	0	—	2	33.33	2	33.33
	S	3	100.00	3	100.00	—	—
Total		5	41.67	9	75.00	4	33.33
Overall	LL	12	40.00	25	83.33	13	43.33
	M	4	26.67	10	66.67	6	40.00
	S	13	86.67	13	86.67	—	—
Total		29	48.33	48	80.00	19	31.67

LL = Landless; M = Marginal Farmers; S = Small Farmers.

In order to obtain the share of different segments of income, the family income per household and per capita income are arranged in ascending order. This series of income is divided into 5 segments of 20 per cent each and the share of each segment is worked out. The data for different categories of households of beneficiary and non-beneficiary are presented in Tables 5.10 and 5.11.

TABLE 5.10: Share of Various Segments in the Family Income

Segments	Percentage of family income							
	Landless		Marginal farmers		Small farmers		Overall	
	A	B	A	B	A	B	A	B
Lower Fifth	10.69	13.33	11.64	13.41	8.93	9.92	10.09	11.96
	(10.69)	(13.33)	(11.64)	(13.41)	(9.93)	(9.92)	(10.09)	(11.96)
Second Fifth	15.59	15.65	15.37	16.53	16.99	16.80	16.16	16.26
	(26.28)	(28.98)	(27.01)	(29.94)	(25.92)	(26.72)	(26.25)	(28.22)
Third Fifth	18.65	17.88	18.04	19.37	20.90	20.14	19.52	19.04
	(44.93)	(46.86)	(45.05)	(49.31)	(46.82)	(46.86)	(45.77)	(47.26)
Fourth Fifth	21.89	21.68	23.47	21.98	24.32	24.64	23.19	22.90
	(66.82)	(68.54)	(68.52)	(71.29)	(71.14)	(71.50)	(68.96)	(70.16)
Top Fifth	33.18	31.46	31.48	28.71	28.86	28.60	31.04	29.84
	(100)	(100)	(100)	(100)	(100)	(100)	(100)	(100)

Note: Figures in brackets are cumulative percentages of family income.
A = Without Scheme Income.
B = With Scheme Income.

TABLE 5.11: Relative Share of Per Capita Family Income of Beneficiaries

Segments	Percentage share in per capita family income							
	Landless		Marginal farmers		Small farmers		Overall	
	A	B	A	B	A	B	A	B
Lower Fifth	10.59	13.13	10.96	10.96	5.35	6.02	8.24	9.78
	(10.59)	(13.13)	(10.96)	(10.96)	(5.35)	(6.02)	(8.24)	(9.78)
Second Fifth	16.13	16.35	15.64	16.07	14.52	14.63	15.31	15.59
	(26.72)	(29.48)	(26.60)	(27.03)	(19.87)	(20.65)	(23.55)	(25.37)
Third Fifth	18.60	18.25	20.82	20.71	19.54	19.95	19.40	19.40
	(45.32)	(47.73)	(47.42)	(47.74)	(39.41)	(40.60)	(42.95)	(44.77)
Fourth Fifth	22.75	21.43	23.05	23.86	25.96	24.92	24.28	23.32
	(68.07)	(69.16)	(70.47)	(71.60)	(65.37)	(65.52	(67.23)	(68.09)
Top Fifth	31.93	30.84	29.53	28.40	34.63	34.48	32.77	31.91
	(100)	(100)	(100)	(100)	(100)	(100)	(100)	(100)

Note: For A, B and parentheses, See Table 5.6.

Beneficiaries

In case of landless households, the poorest 40 per cent households receive only 26 per cent of family income without scheme income and 29 per cent with scheme income. On the other hand, the richest 40 per cent share 55 per cent of the family income without scheme-income and this share becomes 53 per cent with scheme income.

In case of marginal farmers lower 40 per cent households account for 27 per cent and 30 per cent of the family income without and with scheme-income respectively, whereas the upper 40 per cent of the households obtain 55 per cent and 50 per cent.

The concentration of income of small farmers is higher in upper income segments than those of landless and marginal farmers. The pattern of family income without and with scheme income is almost the same. For example, the lower 40 per cent of the small farmers accrue 35 per cent of income, whereas upper 40 per cent account for 53 per cent.

On overall basis, lowest 40 per cent of households claim about 26 per cent of total income without scheme-income and 28 per cent with scheme-income, whereas top 40 per cent households receive 54 per cent and 52 per cent respectively. It is interesting to note that the scheme income has raised the income share of lower 20 per cent households and has eased the concentration of income in the top 20 per cent households.

The analysis of Table 5.11 for per capita income is almost the same.

Lorenz Curve and Gini Concentration Ratio

Based on the above data Lorenz Curves are drawn for both the situations, without scheme income and with scheme income, for all the categories of rural households.

If all incomes are equal, i.e., if every 20 per cent of the households receive 20 per cent of the total income the Lorenz Curve follows the diagonal line of identified households as shown in Figs. 5.1 and 5.2, drawn on the basis of family income and per capita income.

On the Basis of Family Income

Figs. 5.1(a) through 5.1(d) show the inequalities in family income, both with and without scheme-income, as their Lorenz Curves are below the diagonal line. The continuous line represents the distribution of income without scheme income and the broken line presents income with the inclusion of scheme income. In all the four cases, the Lorenz Curve with broken line is closer to the diagonal line than continuous line. It is inferred that the IRDP has lessened the inequalities in the family income of all the categories of households.

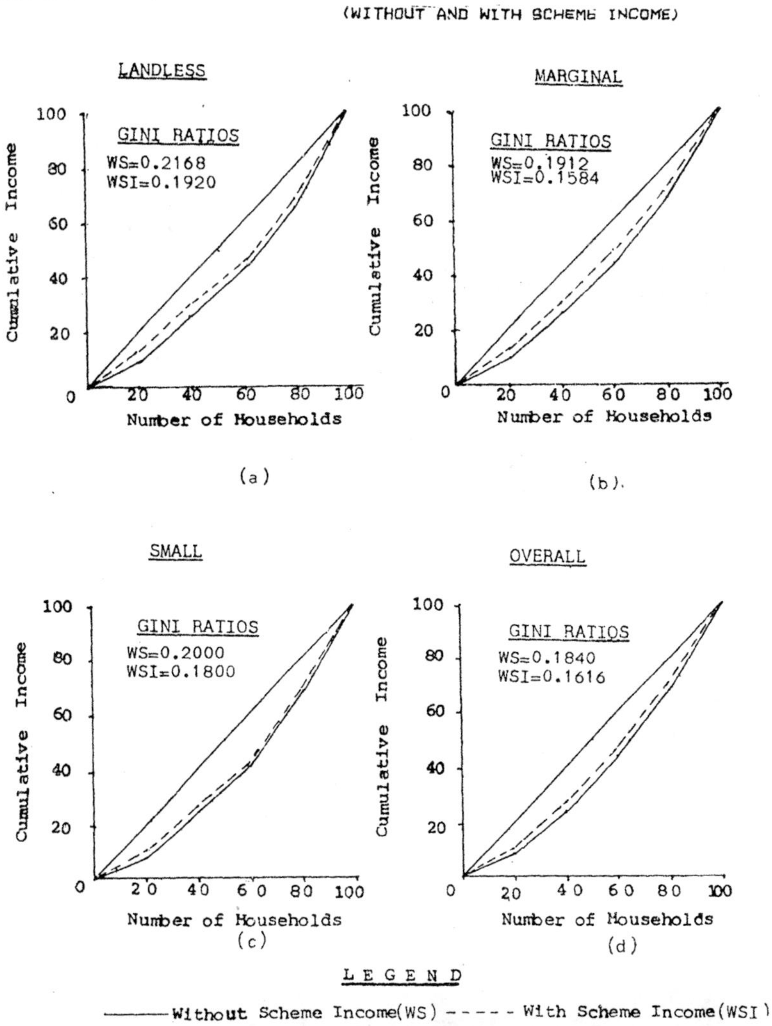

FIG. 5.1: Lorenz Curves Depicting Changes in Family Income Distribution.

In the case of landless households, almost first 50 per cent of the beneficiaries have shown more decrease in the inequalities than the remaining 50 per cent of the households. The Gini Coefficient Ratios for with and without scheme income of landless households are 0.1920 and 0.2168 respectively.

In the case of marginal and small farmers, the inequality in family income has been significantly decreased for the former as compared to the latter. The Gini Ratios for marginal farmers (with and without scheme income) are 0.1584 and. 0.1912, whereas for small farmers these ratios are 0.1800 and 0.2000, respectively.

On the Basis of PCI

The Lorenz Curves drawn for different categories of households on the basis of PCI show almost similar results as in the case of family income, except marginal farmers. It is interesting to note that no reduction in inequalities in income of marginal farmers has been noticed when the Lorenz Curve is drawn on the basis of PCI.

Non-Beneficiaries

The distribution of family income and per capita income by different segments of non-beneficiary household is discussed here for different categories. The results are presented in Table 5.12.

TABLE 5.12: Relative Share of Income of Non-Beneficiary Households

Segments	Landless		Marginal farmers		Small farmers		Overall	
	A	B	A	B	A	B	A	B
Lower Fifth	13.41	11.80	12.69	7.50	10.46	10.32	12.01	10.29
Second Fifth	30.46	25.57	27.88	20.49	28.42	27.49	29.10	25.18
Third Fifth	49.53	42.65	46.44	40.50	47.94	47.22	48.27	43.92
Fourth Fifth	71.82	63.94	71.94	66.24	71.28	69.23	71.61	66.47
Top Fifth	(100)	(100)	(100)	(100)	(100)	(100)	(100)	(100)

Note: A = Cumulative Percentage of Family Income.
B = Cumulative Percentage of Per Capita Family Income.

Lower 40 per cent of the non-beneficiary households receive about 29 per cent of the total family income for all the categories such as landless, marginal and small farmers. The same percentages of households account for 26, 20 and 27 per cent for landless, marginal and small farmers, respectively, on the basis of per capita income. On the other hand, top 40 per cent of these three categories of households obtain 50, 54 and 52 per cent of the family income, but on the basis of per capita income the share of the households is 57, 58 and 53 per cent.

(WITHOUT AND WITH SCHEME INCOME)

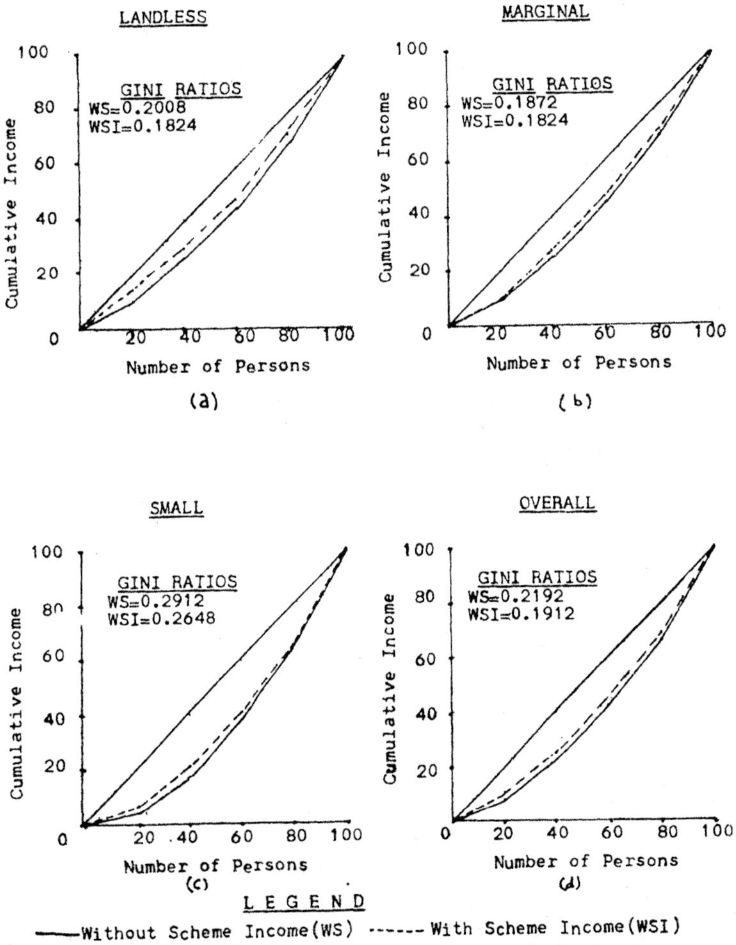

FIG. 5.2: Lorenz Curves Depicting Change in Per Capita Income Distribution.

On the basis of relative shares of income, the Lorenz curves are drawn for different non-beneficiary weaker sections.

On the Basis of Family Income

Figure 5.3 shows the Lorenz curves for landless households, marginal and small farmers. The Lorenz curve of landless households is nearer to the diagonal line than marginal and small farmers. The Lorenz curve of small farmers is farthest from the line of absolute equality. The Gini Ratios for small farmers, marginal farmers and landless households are 0.1872, 0.1792 and 0.1464, respectively.

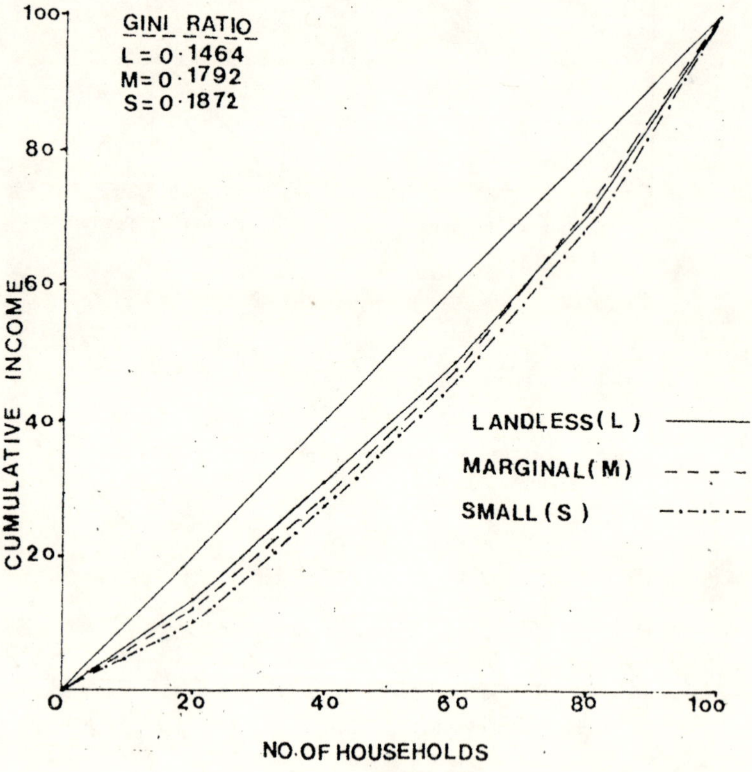

FIG. 5.3: Lorenz Curve Depicting Family Income Distribution Among Non-Beneficiaries.

On the Basis of Per Capita Income

Figure 5.4 is plotted by taking the per capita income distribution. The curve for the small farmers is closer to the line of absolute equality. The Lorenz curve for the marginal farmers is farthest from the diagonal line. Accordingly, the Gini ratios for landless households, marginal and small farmers are 0.2352, 0.2553 and 0.1870, respectively.

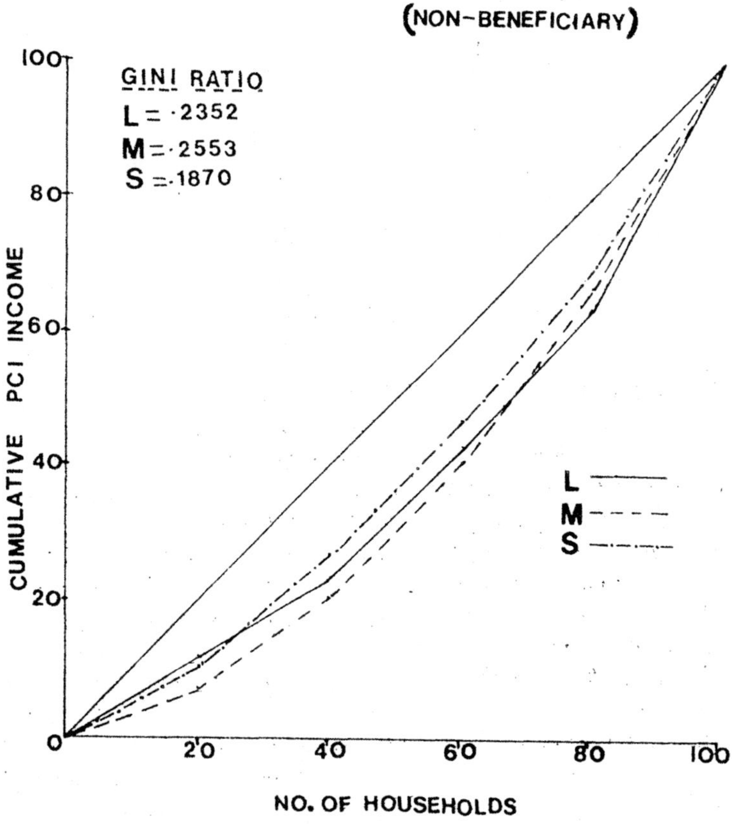

FIG. 5.4: Lorenz Curve showing PCI Distribution.

Quantification of Income Inequality

The quantification of difference in the income inequality between family income with and without scheme income of beneficiaries, and between beneficiaries and non-beneficiaries is presented in Table 5.13. The Standard Deviation of the logarithm of the incomes (SD) and the coefficient of variation (CV) are the two indices of income inequality which are computed and presented here.

TABLE 5.13: Indices of Income Inequality

Category		Beneficiaries				Non-beneficiaries	
		Without scheme income		With scheme income			
		SD*	CV**	SD	CV	SD	CV
Landless	(30)	0.2448	42.68	0.1463	34.14	0.1156	28.13
Landowner	(30)	0.2707	59.40	0.2216	51.39	0.2375	44.71
Marginal	(15)	0.1588	37.88	0.1167	28.51	0.1373	30.26
Small	(15)	0.1954	35.68	0.1778	33.93	0.1710	32.20
Overall	(60)	0.2668	58.76	0.1633	48.51	0.2256	39.13

Note: The figures in parentheses are the sample size.
* SD = Standard Deviation of Log. of Family Income.
** CV = Per cent Coefficient of Variation of Family Income.

Table 5.13 shows that income inequality appears to have dropped by the addition of scheme income in the pre-scheme income of the beneficiaries in terms of both the indices, i.e., SD and CV. The same result is true in case of landless labourers, landowner farmers and all beneficiaries. These results point to the fact that the increase in mean level of income of the target families due to IRDP is associated with the declining income inequality among the beneficiaries. This indicates the higher well-being of the target families and reduction of income inequality due to IRD programme.

The perusal of Table 5.13 shows that the inequalities in income of non-beneficiaries except landless labourers are less than those of beneficiaries in terms of coefficient of variation of income.

It is interesting to note that the income inequalities among beneficiary and non-beneficiary landless labourers are less than landowners. For example, the standard deviation of logarithms of income and coefficient of variation for landless beneficiaries are 0.1463 and 34.14 per cent respectively, whereas these results for landowner beneficiaries are 0.2216 and 51.39 per cent. Similarly, SD and CV for landless non-beneficiaries are much lower than the landowners.

II. DISTRIBUTION OF CONSUMPTION EXPENDITURE

In section I, a detailed analysis of gains and distribution of income among different classes of beneficiary and non-beneficiary households has been presented. In this section, the consumption pattern of different households is discussed. This section seeks to analyse the following issues:

(i) to study per capita consumption expenditure of different groups of households commodity-wise,
(ii) to compute the extent of inequalities between beneficiary and non-beneficiary households; and different groups of families,
(iii) to work-out the people living below poverty line defined in terms of minimum per capita expenditure.

In this study, consumer expenditure comprises all expenditure incurred by any household exclusively on domestic account, including consumption out of home grown products. A series of tables given in subsequent pages represent the value of consumption of broad groups of items per person for a period of twelve months. About 15 main items are considered for the purposes of study. These items are:

(1) Cereals;
(2) Pulses;
(3) Milk and its products;
(4) Meat, egg and fish;
(5) Vegetables and fruits;
(6) Sugar and Gur;
(7) Miscellaneous (includes all other food items which are not included above);
(8) Clothing;
(9) Fuel and light;
(10) Durable consumer goods;
(11) Intoxicants;
(12) Expenditure on education;
(13) Medicine;
(14) Travelling; and
(15) Social ceremonies.

The items from one to seven constitute 'All Food Items' and from eight to fifteen as 'Non-Food Items'.

Seven expenditure groups on the basis of per capita consumption are constituted for the purpose of analysis of distribution of consumption expenditure. The lowest and the highest per capita expenditure groups are less than Rs.600 and Rs.2,400 and above. The household with less than Rs.600 of consumption expenditure is called as 'destitute'. An attempt has also been made to estimate people below poverty line on the basis of per capita consumption expenditure. For the purpose of this study, the yearly per capita expenditure of Rs.1,080 is taken as cut-off point, i.e., the household below this level of expenditure is considered as below poverty line.

Per Capita Expenditure of Beneficiary and Non-Beneficiary

Table 5.14 gives per capita expenditure commodity-wise and their percentage share with beneficiaries and non-beneficiaries.

The perusal of Table 5.14 shows that about 63 per cent of per capita consumption expenditure of the beneficiaries is spent on food items, viz., cereals, pulses, milk and its products, meat and fish etc. The consumption expenditure of small farmers is more than those of landless households and marginal farmers. The per capita expenditure of landholders (marginal and small) of milk and its products, vegetables and fruits is higher than the landless households. Per capita expenditure on clothing also increases with the beneficiary landowners as compared with landless households. It is observed that landless households spend only 0.66 per cent or Rs.8 per head per annum on education, whereas marginal and small farmers spend 1.11 and 3.16 per cent of the total consumption expenditure respectively. The expenditure on medicine and fuel and light shows the similar trend for landholders and landless.

The non-beneficiary households spend 64 per cent of the total expenditure on food items. Table 5.14 shows that the major share (31%) of the total expenditure of the non-beneficiaries is taken away by cereals. The next important item is milk and its products. The pattern of expenditure of landless and marginal farmers is almost the same, i.e., they spend 31 and 37 per cent on cereals respectively. But the small farmers incur only 24 per cent of the total expenditure on this item. Non-beneficiary households spend 20 per cent of the total expenditure on clothing. It is observed that per capita expenditure of marginal farmers is much higher than small farmers. It is mainly due to the high expenditure of marginal farmers on cereals compared with their other counterparts.

TABLE 5.14: Per Capita Annual Consumption Expenditure of Beneficiaries and Non-Beneficiaries

(Rupees)

Sl. No.	Items	Landless		Marginal		Small		Overall	
		B	NB	B	NB	B	NB	B	NB
1 2	3	4	5	6	7	8	9	10	
1.	Cereals	320 (26.06)	340 (31.11)	348 (27.57)	520 (36.90)	349 (20.84)	433 (26.67)	334 (24.36)	430 (31.36)
2.	Pulses	84 (6.84)	79 (7.23)	85 (6.74)	100 (5.94)	99 (5.91)	88 (5.42)	88 (6.42)	86 (6.27)
3.	Milk & Milk Products	135 (10.99)	100 (9.15)	149 (11.81)	197 (11.71)	276 (16.48)	190 (11.71)	166 (12.11)	146 (10.65)
4.	Meat, Egg & Fish	40 (3.26)	20 (1.83)	6 (0.48)	26 (1.54)	40 (2.39)	21 (1.29)	32 (2.33)	22 (1.60)
5.	Veg. & Fruits	56 (4.56)	43 (3.43)	58 (4.60)	91 (5.41)	99 (5.91)	79 (4.87)	67 (4.89)	64 (4.67)
6	Sugar	104 (8.46)	101 (9.15)	105 (8.32)	144 (8.56)	136 (8.12)	130 (8.01)	115 (8.39)	118 (8.61)
7.	Misc.	33 (2.69)	41 (3.75)	41 (3.24)	56 (3.32)	56 (3.34)	55 (3.39)	41 (2.99)	48 (3.50)
Sub Total 1 to 7		772 (62.87)	723 (66.15)	792 (62.76)	1051 (62.45)	1046 (62.44)	996 (61.37)	843 (61.48)	872 (63.60)

Contd.

TABLE 5.14 *Contd.*

1	2	3	4	5	6	7	8	9	10
8.	Fuel & Light	49 (3.99)	47 (4.30)	72 (5.71)	17 (1.01)	96 (5.73)	102 (6.28)	92 (6.71)	72 (5.25)
9.	Clothing	242 (19.71)	213 (19.49)	287 (22.74)	360 (21.39)	307 (18.33)	293 (18.05)	270 (19.69)	268 (19.55)
10.	Durable Goods	4 (0.33)	9 (0.82)	5 (0.40)	6 (0.36)	3 (0.68)	5 (0.31)	3 (0.22)	7 (0.51)
11.	Intoxicants	21 (1.71)	16 (0.46)	14 (1.11)	16 (0.95)	23 (1.37)	50 (3.08)	20 (1.46)	25 (1.82)
12.	Education	8 (0.66)	8 (0.73)	14 (1.11)	19 (1.13)	53 (3.16)	30 (1.83)	21 (1.46)	16 (1.17)
13.	Medicine	49 (3.99)	24 (2.20)	39 (3.09)	73 (4.39)	72 (4.30)	75 (4.62)	49 (3.57)	45 (3.50)
14.	Travelling	43 3.50)	28 (2.56)	39 (3.09)	59 (3.50)	70 (4.18)	71 (4.37)	49 (3.57)	47 (3.49)
15.	Social Ceremonies	40 (3.26)	25 (2.29)	-	6 (0.36)	6 (0.36)	2 (0.12)	24 (1.75)	14 (1.02)
Sub Total 8 to 15		456 (37.13)	370 (33.85)	470 (37.24)	632 (37.55)	629 (37.55)	627 (38.63)	528 (38.51)	498 (36.40)
G. Total		1228 (100)	1093 (100)	1262 (100)	1683 (100)	1675 (100)	1623 (100)	1371 (100)	1370 (100)

Note: Figures in parentheses are percentages.

All the beneficiaries except marginal farmers have higher per capita expenditure than the non-beneficiaries. This indicates that beneficiary landless and small farmers have acquired a better standard of living than non-beneficiaries of the same categories. The high percentage expenditure on non-food items of beneficiaries reveals better quality of life than those of non-beneficiaries.

The pattern of expenditure of beneficiary and non-beneficiary households is almost similar. Among food items, cereals and milk and its products constitute major share of consumption expenditure of all categories of selected beneficiary and non-beneficiary households. Among the non-food items, clothing, fuel and light and medicine account for major share of total expenditure. There is no significant difference in consumption pattern between beneficiaries and non-beneficiaries. It is evident from this analysis that IRD programme has not changed the priorities of consumption of the beneficiaries as compared to non-beneficiaries.

Distribution of Consumption Expenditure

Beneficiary Households

Appendix A through Appendix H give a breakdown of consumption expenditure for different expenditure groups of beneficiaries and non-beneficiaries. The consumers are divided into seven expenditure classes beginning with those who spend less than Rs.600 per capita per annum and go up to the top class spending above Rs.2,400. It is observed from the tables that there is no beneficiary household having per capita expenditure less than Rs.600. It points to the fact that there is no destitute among the selected beneficiaries. It is also evident from the tables that no landless and marginal farmer has consumption more than Rs.2,499. The concentration of beneficiary landless and marginal farmers is in consumption expenditure group of Rs.1,080 and Rs.1,500, and of small farmers is in Rs.1,800 and Rs.2,400. Only nine per cent of the small farmers fall in the expenditure group of Rs.2,400 and above.

The average expenditure of landless on cereals is between Rs.282 to Rs.425 for different expenditure classes, whereas this is between Rs.253 to Rs.480 for marginal farmers and between Rs.200 to Rs.489 for small farmers. The percentage expenditure on cereals is estimated to fall gradually with the rise in expenditure class of overall beneficiaries, i.e., from 33 per cent in the lowest class to 19 per cent in the top expenditure class. All other food items show an increasing trend in the initial stage, then remains constant and falls afterwards. It is evident from Appendix D that the average expenditure on food items increases when we go up the consumption expenditure ladder. But the percentage expenditure decreases with the increase in per capita expenditure on food-items.

For non-food items, the proportion of expenditure on fuel and light, education and medicine has an increasing trend. The per cent expenditure on these items is rising with the rise in average expenditure. If we consider expenditure of less than Rs.1,080 as below poverty line expenditure then 27 per cent persons (but 20 per cent households) come under this category according to per capita consumption expenditure.

Non-Beneficiary Households

The per capita consumption expenditure classes of various categories of households are presented in Appendix E to Appendix H. such as beneficiary households, no non-beneficiary household is in the consumption expenditure group of less than Rs.600. It shows that no destitute is found in the sample households of Punjab State. It is also observed that there is no marginal farmer and small farmer having consumption expenditure less than Rs.840 and Rs.1,080 respectively. It is evident from these figures that standard of living of marginal and small farmers is better than landless beneficiary households.

Appendix H shows that the average expenditure on cereals increases with the higher expenditure groups, but the proportion of this item in total expenditure represents a declining trend. Similarly, proportionate share of expenditure on foodgrains decreases with the increase in consumption expenditure.

For non-food items, the money expenditure of these items rises, but their percentage share in total expenditure goes up in the beginning and then declines with the rise in expenditure group. The main items of expenditure are cereals and clothing with all the classes of weaker sections. The majority of landless non-beneficiary households fall in the expenditure group of Rs.840 and Rs.1,080, whereas the concentration of marginal and small farmers is in Rs.1,800 to Rs.2,400 and Rs.1,080 to Rs.1,500, respectively.

Concentration of Consumption Expenditure

For analysing the distribution of consumption expenditure among the various strata of households, the households are arranged into 20 per cent groups in ascending order of their per capita expenditure. The percentage of per capita consumption of 20 per cent of households is shown in Table 5.15. Table 5.15 shows the concentration of consumption expenditure in landless and landowner beneficiary and non-beneficiary households.

TABLE 5.15: Percentage Distribution of Consumption Expenditure According to the 20 per cent of Households

Segments	Landless households		Landowner households	
	B	NB	B	NB
Bottom 20 per cent	14.00	14.83	12.08	13.56
	(14.00)	(14.83)	(12.08)	(13.56)
Second 20 per cent	17.56	16.68	16.01	16.45
	(31.56)	(31.51)	(28.09)	(30.01)
Third 20 per cent	19.26	18.03	19.43	19.84
	(50.82)	(49.54)	(47.52)	(49.85)
Fourth 20 per cent	22.19	22.02	23.33	22.57
	(73.01)	(71.56)	(70.85)	(72.42)
Top 20 per cent	26.99	28.44	29.15	27.58
	(100)	(100)	(100)	(100)

Note: The figures in brackets are cumulative percentages.
B = Beneficiary Households.
NB = Non-Beneficiary Households.

The perusal of Table 5.15 shows that there exists inequality of consumption expenditure among different 20 per cent beneficiary and non-beneficiary households. It is evident from Table 5.15 that there occur greater inequalities among landless non-beneficiary households than beneficiary households. The landowner non-beneficiary farmers represent more even distribution of consumption expenditure than those of beneficiary farmers. For example, bottom 40 per cent beneficiary and non-beneficiary landowner households claim a share of 28 and 30 per cent of the total expenditure, respectively, whereas top 40 per cent households account for 52 per cent and 50 per cent, respectively.

Lorenz Curve and Gini Ratio

The above discussion shows that there exists inequality in consumption expenditure among beneficiary and non-beneficiary households. In order to have a clear idea of consumption distribution among different households, the Lorenz Curves are drawn for the data presented in Table 5.15.

Figures 5.5 and 5.6, on the horizontal line cumulative percentage of households and on vertical axis cumulative percentage of consumption expenditure of different beneficiary and non-beneficiary households has been shown. All the Lorenz Curves are away from the line of equal distribution. Figure 5.5 shows that the consumption distribution of first 60 per cent landless households is almost similar, but this distribution for remaining 40 per cent is less skewed for beneficiaries as compared with non-beneficiaries.

Figure 5.6 shows that the Lorenz Curve of non-beneficiary landowner households is closer to the line of equal distribution than that of beneficiary households. It points out that the consumption expenditure is more evenly distributed among non-beneficiary landowners than that of beneficiaries.

The magnitude of consumption inequalities has been worked out by Gini concentration ratio. This ratio is calculated by dividing the area of the curve below the line of absolute equality by the area of right angled triangle. The Gini ratios for landless beneficiary and non-beneficiary households are 0.1304 and 0.1392, respectively, whereas these ratios for landowner households of both the categories are 0.1912 and 0.1624. This points to the fact that the magnitude of inequalities in consumption expenditure for landless is lower than the landowner households of both beneficiaries and non-beneficiaries. It is observed that the beneficiary landless households and non-beneficiary landowner households show less inequalities in consumption expenditure than their counterparts.

III. TOTAL ASSETS OF TARGET GROUP HOUSEHOLDS AND THEIR DISTRIBUTION AMONG DIFFERENT CLASSES OF HOUSEHOLDS BY ASSET GROUPS

The study of distribution of size and pattern of assets holding by the households acquires special economic importance. This would throw light on the capacity to generate income and size of wealth of different households. The total value of assets includes the value of items, viz.,

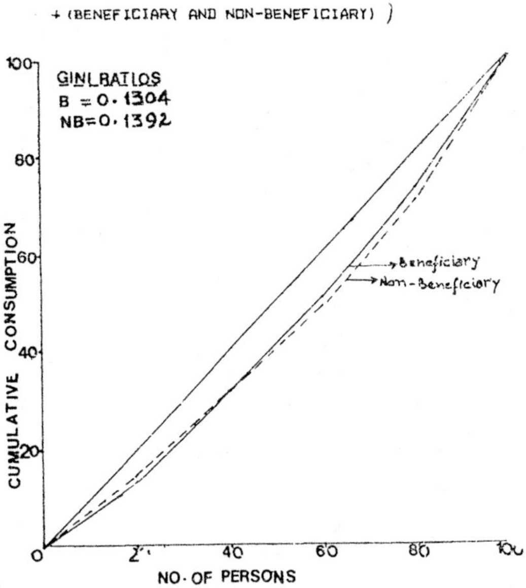

FIG. 5.5: Lorenz Curves Depicting Distribution of Consumption — Landless.

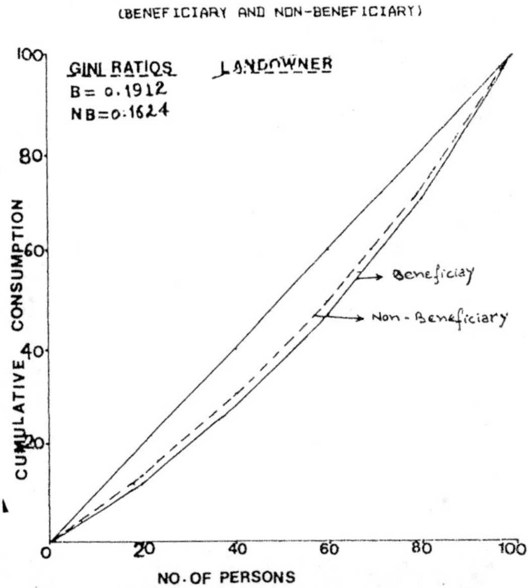

FIG. 5.6: Lorenz Curves Depicting Distribution Consumption — Landowner.

land, farm implements, livestock,[8] bullocks and bullock carts, and durable household assets.[9] Farm equipments are further classified into mechanical and non-mechanical. Mechanical implements include tractor, pump-set, tubewells, thresher, etc. The physical assets are valued at the current market price.

The average value of total assets per household for beneficiaries and non-beneficiaries has been presented in Table 5.16. The table shows that the livestock is one of the most important components of the total assets for beneficiary landless households, whereas land occupies the greatest attention of the landholders. Next important item of total assets is livestock with beneficiary landowners. The major share of land in the total assets points to the fact that landholders have an edge over landless for income generation. The landless households get benefits only through dairy business, whereas the farming and dairy business are the most important for small and marginal farmers.

The contribution of IRDP in total assets of the household is considerable. The beneficiary landless and marginal farmers have the major part of the livestock asset under income generation scheme of the programme. It has already been made clear that the majority of the beneficiary households purchase milch animal out of the loan from the banks in the study area. The average amount invested in livestock is estimated to be Rs.3,518 and Rs.4,420 for beneficiary landless and marginal farmers, respectively. Mechanical inputs are the most important assets for beneficiary small farmers.

These farmers have got tube-wells/pumpsets under IRDP. Therefore, the investment of small farmers in modern inputs is much higher than marginal farmers.

Table 5.16 presents the analysis regarding the composition of assets of non-beneficiary households. Here the structure of assets of non-beneficiary households shows a different tendency as compared with beneficiary households. For example, livestock and family assets are two most important assets for landless households. Land constitutes a major portion of total assets for landowner non-beneficiaries. The share of land varies between 87 and 93 per cent in the total assets. Its importance increases with the increase in size of holdings. The share of total agricultural assets (Land + implements + Bullock & Bullock Cart) is between 93 per cent and 97 per cent of the total value of asset with the farmers.

TABLE 5.16: Composition of Assets Household

(Rupees)

Category	Land	Implements		Bullock & bullock cart	Livestock	Non-agri. Business assets	H.H. assets	Total with land	Total without land
		Mech.	Non.Mech.						
1	2	3	4	5	6	7	8	9	10
Beneficiary									
Landless	—	—	—	—	3518 (70.52)	70 (1.40)	1401 (27.08)	4989 (100)	4989 (100)
Marginal	55066 (84.45)	417 (0.64)	330 (0.51)	2833 (4.34)	4420 (6.78)	10 (0.02)	2125 (3.26)	65202 (100)	10135 (15.55)
Small	126867 (87.63)	4553 (3.14)	527 (0.36)	2700 (1.86)	4687 (3.24)	1533 (1.00)	3918 (2.71)	144784 (100)	17917 (12.37)
Overall	45484 (82.51)	1243 (2.26)	215 (0.39)	1383 (2.51)	4035 (7.34)	420 (0.76)	2211 (4.02)	54991 (100)	9507 (17.29)
Non-Beneficiary									
Landless	—	—	—	—	1238 (52.77)	—	1108 (46.56)	2346 (100)	2346 (100)
Marginal	49600 (87.31)	497 (0.88)	267 (0.46)	2533 (4.50)	2273 (14.03)	—	1587 (2.82)	56757 (100)	7157 (12.69)
Small	108027 (93.14)	883 (0.76)	427 (0.37)	3367 (2.93)	1400 (1.21)	—	1936 (1.60)	116080 (100)	7973 (6.86)
Overall	39417 (88.75)	345 (0.78)	173 (0.36)	1475 (3.32)	1537 (3.51)	—	1415 (3.20)	44380 (100)	4963 (11.22)

Note: Figures in parentheses are percentages to total.

It is evident from the above analysis that pattern of distribution of assets among the cultivators is dominated by the nature of distribution of land amongst them. The importance of mechanical as well as non-mechanical inputs increases with the size of holding. The value of assets, therefore, is broadly indicative of the size of farm business of cultivator households. The skewness of distribution of assets becomes more vivid if we consider the agricultural labourers separately. All the landless households have average value of assets, i.e., less than Rs.5,500. Data presented above, clearly point to the fact that the economic status enjoyed by the landholders, adjudged on the basis of their place in asset group, is far superior to that of landless households.

There is significant difference in the pattern of assets between beneficiary and non-beneficiary households. The livestock asset is important for beneficiary landless and marginal farmers (apart from land), whereas it is not so with their non-beneficiary counterparts. As against the average value of livestock asset of Rs.3,518 and Rs.4,420 for beneficiary landless and marginal farmers respectively, the average value for this item is only Rs.1,238 and Rs.2,273 for the non-beneficiary counterparts. The per household investment on mechanical inputs of beneficiary small farmers is Rs.4,553 as against only Rs.883 for non-beneficiaries of the same farm size. This difference is largely due to the purchase of assets with assistance of IRDP by the beneficiaries. Beneficiary landless households and marginal farmers mainly undertook investment in milch animals, whereas small farmers invested in the purchase of mechanical inputs.

Distribution of Total Assets According to Asset Groups

The distribution of total assets according to asset-groups reveals the concentration of the proportion of households and the value of assets in the various groups. A relatively high share of assets of households in the top asset group might generally indicate relatively high average value of assets per household and greater inequality within the sample households. Correspondingly, low share of assets of such households might indicate relatively low average level of assets per household and greater equality in distribution of assets within the selected households.

For the purpose of analysis of the distribution of assets among beneficiary and non-beneficiary landless and landowner categories of households, the distribution of assets of these classes is compiled in two ways:

(i) by excluding land asset and dividing the total assets into seven groups starting from less than Rs.2,500 and ending with Rs.50,000 and above,

(ii) by including land asset and dividing the total assets into 10 groups, the lowest and the highest asset group being less than Rs.5,000 and Rs.1.5 lakh and above, respectively.

The results are presented in Tables 5.17 and 5.18.

Distribution of Assets — Without Land

Table 5.17 shows that the average value of assets of overall beneficiaries is Rs.9,507 compared with Rs.4,962 of the non-beneficiaries. The average value of assets rises as the size of asset group increases. This increase is more uniform in case of non-beneficiaries than in the case of beneficiaries.

The concentration of landless beneficiary households falls in asset group of Rs.2,500 and Rs.5,000, and that of non-beneficiaries is confined to the asset group up to Rs.2,500. The concentration of beneficiaries in the high asset group is mainly due to inclusion of IRDP's assisted assets. As against average value of assets of beneficiary landless households of Rs.4,989, the average value of the assets of landless non-beneficiary households is Rs.2,346 only.

The position of beneficiary and non-beneficiary marginal farmers is better than the landless. It is observed that the asset groups start from Rs.5,000 in case of former and from Rs.2,500 in case of latter. The concentration of beneficiary marginal farmers falls in the asset groups of Rs.5,000 to Rs.7,500 and Rs.7,500 to Rs.10,000, whereas it is limited to the asset group of Rs.5,000 and Rs.7,500 in case of non-beneficiary counterparts. Average value of asset per marginal farmer is Rs.10,135 as compared with Rs.7,157 of non-beneficiary marginal farmer.

TABLE 5.17: Average Value of Assets of Beneficiaries and Non-Beneficiaries

(Without Land)

Asset Group (Rs.)	Landless		Marginal		Small		Overall	
	No.	Av. Value	No.	Av. Value	No.	Av. Value	No.	Av. Value
Beneficiary								
Upto 2500	1	1200	-	-	-	-	1	1200
	(3.33)	(0.80)					(1.67)	(0.21)
2500 -5000	17	4107	-	-	-	-	17	4107
	(56.67)	(46.65)					(28.33)	(12.24)
5000 -7500	10	5885	2	6325	-	-	12	5958
	(33.33)	(39.32)	(13.33	(8.32)			(20.00)	(12.53)
7500 -10000	1	7900	8	9346	2	9049	11	9161
	(3.33)	(5.28)	(53.33)	(49.19)	(13.33)	(6.73)	(18.33)	(17.67)
10000 -15000	1	11800	4	11200	7	12193	12	11829
	(3.33)	(7.95)	(26,67)	(29.27)	(46.67)	(31.76)	(20.00)	(24.88)
15000 -20000	-	-	1	19800	3	16850	4	17587
			(6.67)	(13.02)	(20.00)	(18.81)	(6.67)	(12.33)
20000 & above	-	-	-	-	3	38250	3	38250
					(20.00)	(42.70)	(5.00)	(20.72)
Overall	30	4989	15	10135	15	17917	60	9507
	(100)	(100)	(100)	(100)	(100)	(100)	(100)	(100)

Non-Beneficiary

Asset Group (Rs.)	Landless		Marginal		Small		Overall	
	No.	Av. Value	No.	Av. Value	No.	Av. Value	No.	Av. Value
Upto -2500	20 (66.67)	1746 (49.70)	-	-	-	-	20 (33.33)	1746 (11.73)
2500 -5000	9 (30.00)	3367 (43.13)	1 (6.67)	3175 (3.02)	-	-	10 (16.67)	3348 (11.25)
5000 -7500	1 (3.33)	5050 (7.18)	9 (66.67)	6048 (57.94)	8 (53.33)	6274 (41.93)	18 (30.00)	6093 (36.84)
7500 -10000	-	-	3 (13.33)	8750 (16.82)	3 (20.00)	8250 (20.68)	68500 (10.00)	(17.13)
10000 -15000	-	-	2 (13.33)	11700 (22.23)	4 (26.67)	11312 (37.39)	6 (10.00)	11442 (23.06)
Overall	30 (100)	2346 (100)	15 (100)	7157 (100)	15 (100)	7973 (100)	60 (100)	4963 (100)

Note: Figures in parentheses are percentages to total.

The concentration of beneficiary small farmers is observed in the asset groups of Rs.10,000 and Rs.15,000, whereas in the case of non-beneficiaries of the same group, the concentration is restricted to the asset group of Rs.5,000 to Rs.7,500. The greater concentration of beneficiary small farmers in higher asset group than other selected households points towards the better economic condition of that class.

It is observed from the above analysis that economic condition of landholders is much better than the landless. Investment made under IRDP schemes has improved the asset group of beneficiaries as compared to non-beneficiaries. The analysis for overall sample households shows that most of the beneficiaries own assets in the asset group of Rs.2,500 and Rs.5,000, whereas the concentration of non-beneficiaries remains in the first group of asset, i.e., up to Rs.2,500.

Distribution of Assets including Land

Land is always very important asset with farmers and the most valuable among the assets of the cultivator families, therefore, the analysis of the total assets should also include the value of land, which is owned by a household other than house site or a vacant land. The results are presented in Table 5.18.

Beneficiary Households

The perusal of Table 5.18 shows that 30 per cent of the beneficiaries falling in the asset groups below Rs.5000 own only 2.15 per cent of the total value of assets. The richest asset groups, i.e., over Rs.1.20 lakh account for only 20 per cent of the households but they hold 56.5 per cent of the total assets.

TABLE 5.18: Distribution of Households and Value of Assets held by Beneficiaries and Non-Beneficiaries According to Asset Groups.

Asset group (Rs.)	Beneficiaries				Non-Beneficiaries			
	Landless		Land-owners		Landless		Land-owners	
	No.	Av.Value	No.	Av.Value	No.	Av.Value	No.	Av.Value
1	2	3	4	5	6	7	8	9
Upto 2500	1 (3.33)	1200 (0.80)	-	-	20 (66.67)	1746 (49.62)	-	-
2500 - 5000	17 (56.67)	4107 (46.63)	-	-	10 (33.33)	3545 (50.37)	-	-
5000 - 7500	10 (33.33)	5885 (39.31)	-	-	-	-	-	-
7500 - 15000	2 (6.67)	9900 (13.26)	-	-	-	-	-	-
15000 - 40000	-	-	1 (3.33)	39800 (1.26)	-	-	4 (13.33)	28737 (4.43)
40000 - 65000	-	-	5 (16.67)	55780 (8.85)	-	-	3 (10.00)	49552 (5.74)
65000 - 90000			9 (30.00)	73258 (20.95)	-	-	9 (30.00)	74017 (25.70)
90000 - 120000	-	-	3 (10.00)	102550 (9.77)	-	-	8 (26.67)	102949 (31.76)
120000 - 150000	-	-	6 (20.00)	135704 (25.85)	-	-	5 (16.67)	137530 (26.53)
150000 & above	-	-	6 (20.00)	174980 (33.35)	-	-	1 (3.33)	151450 (5.48)
Overall	30 (100)	4989 (100)	30 (100)	104995 (100)	30 (100)	2346 (100)	30 (100)	86415 (100)

Note: Figures in the parentheses of average value of assets represent the percentages of the total asset.

The inequality in the holding of assets is noticed in the case of both landless and landowner households in varying degree. No landowner is found having assets less than Rs.15,000. It is observed that 20 per cent of landowner households falling in the asset groups of Rs.15,000 and Rs.65,000 account for only 10 per cent of total assets. At the other end of the distribution, 20 per cent of households owning assets of Rs.1.50 lakh and above have as high as 33.35 per cent of the value of total assets.

Landless labourers whose asset holding is far less than landholders are the poorest. It is observed that there is no beneficiary landless household having assets more than Rs.15,000. It may be noted that 60 per cent of landless households in the asset groups less than Rs.5,000 have 47 per cent of the total assets.

Non-Beneficiary Households

Similar trend of inequalities in the distribution of assets is found for non-beneficiaries. The perusal of Table 5.18 shows that 50 per cent of non-beneficiaries falling in the asset groups of less than Rs.5,000 account for 2.64 per cent households. At the extreme end of the distribution, 10 per cent of the households having assets more than Rs.1.20 lakh own 31.52 per cent of the total value of assets.

No non-beneficiary landowner has asset holding less than Rs.15,000. Twenty three per cent of the landholders fall in the asset group of Rs.15,000 and Rs.65,000 and own 10 per cent of the total value of assets. On the other extreme, top 20 per cent of the households account for 32 per cent of the total assets.

All the landless households fall in the asset groups of less than Rs.5,000. It shows the poor economic position of the non-beneficiaries.

The average asset holding of non-beneficiaries is much smaller than beneficiaries. The impact of IRDP on asset holding of beneficiaries is vital. The above discussion points to the existence of inequality in the holding of assets by different classes of weaker sections. For measuring the inequalities between beneficiaries and non-beneficiaries Lorenz Curves and Gini Concentration Ratios are also used.

Relative Position of Each of the Assets to Total Assets Holding

The main asset item of landholders is land. It is found that the share of land component in the total assets as one moved from lower to the higher asset group increases, particularly up to the asset group of Rs.90,000 and Rs.1.20 lakh for beneficiaries and from Rs.1.20 lakh to Rs.1.50 lakh for non-beneficiaries.

Land accounts for 50 to 91 per cent (Table 5.19) for beneficiaries and from 75 to 92 per cent for non-beneficiaries of different asset groups. Land is continued to be the most important single item of the assets of the farmers. It is observed that the percentage share of land is higher in case of non-beneficiaries than beneficiaries. It shows that land is the major income generating asset with non-beneficiaries. Next important item is livestock which accounts for over two-thirds of the total assets for beneficiary landless and 3 to 21 for landholders. For non-beneficiaries, livestock is not so important. It is interesting to note that the share of livestock in total assets decreases with the increase in asset group for beneficiaries.

The trend of proportion of farm implements in total assets with different asset groups for both beneficiaries and non-beneficiaries is absurd. But it is obvious that implements are more important for beneficiaries than non-beneficiaries in all the size groups.

The average value of assets rises as the size of asset group increases. Livestock is observed as the most important asset for landless beneficiaries. The importance of this asset is second to land asset for farmers.

Lorenz Curves and Gini Ratios

On the basis of Table 5.19 the Lorenz Curves are drawn for beneficiary and non-beneficiary households. The cumulative percentages of households of different segments have been taken on horizontal axis and cumulative percentages of assets on vertical axis. Lorenz Curves of both beneficiary and non-beneficiary households are farther from the line of absolute equal distribution. This shows the unequal distribution of assets among beneficiaries and non-beneficiaries. The Lorenz Curves of both the categories intersect each other. This is indicative of the fact that first 75 per cent of the non-beneficiaries represent larger inequalities than beneficiaries, but remaining 25 per cent households show the reverse, i.e., lesser inequalities in the distribution of assets among non-beneficiaries than beneficiaries. The Gini Ratios for these two categories are almost same, i.e., 0.5937 and 0.5905 (Fig. 5.7).

TABLE 5.19: Assets of Beneficiaries and Non-Benficiaries Per Household according to Asset Groups in Study Area

(Rupees)

Asset group (Rs.)	No. of households	Land	Implements	Bullock cart	Livestock	Non agri. business assets	Households assets	Total
Beneficiary								
Upto - 2500	1	-	-	-	-	-	1200	1200
	(1.67)						(100)	(100)
2500 - 5000	17	-	-	-	2965	88	1054	4107
	(28.33)				(72.19)	(2.14)	(25.67)	(100)
5000 - 7500	10	-	-	-	4015	-	1870	5885
	(16.67)				(68.22)		(31.78)	(100)
7500 - 15000	2	-	-	-	7500	300	2125	9925
	(3.33)				(75.57)	(3.02)	(21.41)	(100)
15000 - 40000	1	20000	750	4000	8200	-	6850	39800
	(1.67)	(50.25)	(1.88)	(10.05)	(20.60)		(17.21)	(100)
40000 - 65000	5	45800	550	3000	4840	-	1590	55780
	(8.33)	(82.11)	(0.99)	(5.38)	(8.67)		(2.85)	(100)
65000 - 90000	9	64111	856	2611	3767	17	1892	73254
	(15.11)	(87.52)	(1.17)	(3.56)	(5.14)	(0.02)	(2.58)	(100)
90000 - 120000	3	91333	2167	2667	3833	-	3825	103825
	(5.00)	(87.97)	(2.09)	(2.56)	(3.69)		(3.68)	(100)
120000 - 150000	6	112333	7891	1750	5383	3333	5012	135702
	(10.00)	(82.70)	(5.81)	(12.90)	(3.97)	(2.46)	(3.69)	(100)
150000 & above	6	159167	3725	3667	4416	500	3505	274980
	(10.00)	(90.96)	(2.13)	(2.10)	(2.52)	(0.29)	(2.00)	(100)

Asset group (Rs.)	No. of households	Land	Implements	Bullock cart	Livestock	Non agri. business assets	Households assets	Total
Overall	60 (100)	45484 (82.72)	1458 (2.76)	1383 (2.52)	4035 (7.30)	420 (10.67)	2211 (4.03)	54991 (100)
Non-Beneficiary								
Upto - 2500	20 (33.33)	-	-	-	637 (36.48)	-	1109 (63.52)	1746 (100)
2500 - 5000	10 (16.67)	-	-	-	2440 (68.83)	-	1105 (31.17)	3545 (100)
5000 - 7500	-	-	-	-	-	-	-	-
7500 - 15000	-	-	-	-	-	-	-	-
15000 - 40000	4 (6.67)	21500 (74.82)	725 (2.52)	2000 (6.96)	2125 (7.39)	-	2387 (8.31)	28737 (100)
40000 - 65000	3 (5.00)	44333 (89.46)	417 (0.84)	2000 (4.04)	1767 (3.57)	-	1035 (2.09)	49352 (100)
65000 - 90000	9 (15.00)	66111 (89.32)	889 (1.20)	3111 (4.20)	2478 (13.35)	-	1428 (1.93)	74017 (100)
90000 - 120000	8 (13.33)	95125 (92.40)	1513 (1.47)	3000 (2.92)	1450 (1.41)	-	1861 (1.81)	102949 (100)
120000 - 150000	5 (8.33)	130000 (94.52)	1110 (0.80)	3600 (2.62)	880 (0.64)	-	1940 (1.41)	137530 (100)
150000 & Above	1 (1.67)	140000 (92.44)	1200 (0.79)	4500 (2.97)	3000 (1.98	-	2750 (1.82)	151450 (100)
Overall	60 (100)	39417 (88.75)	518 (1.14)	1475 (3.32)	1537 (3.51)	-	1415 (3.20)	44300 (100)

Note: Figures in parentheses are percentage of the total.

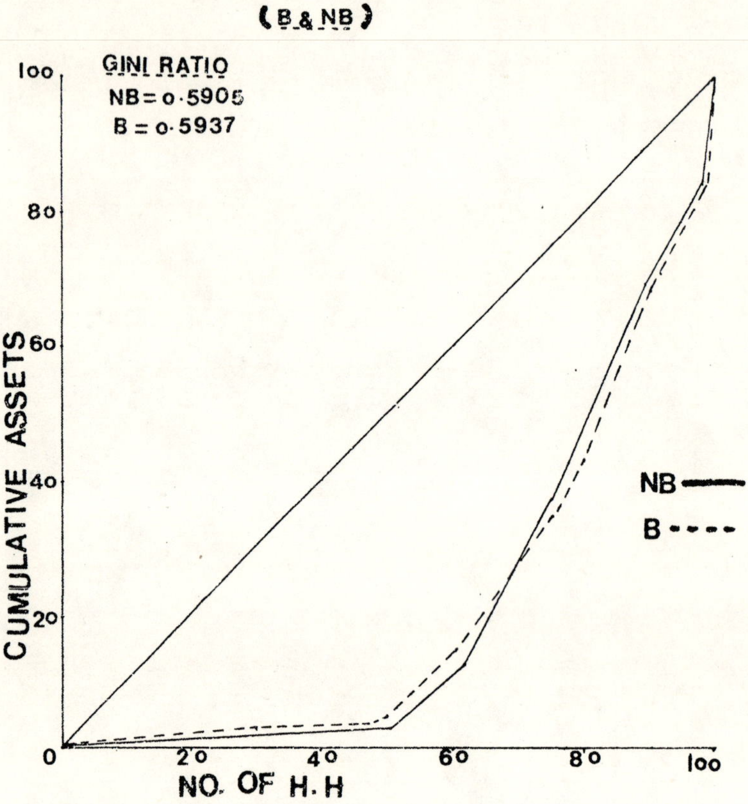

FIG. 5.7: Lorenz Curves showing Distribution of Assets

IV. EMPLOYMENT OF LABOUR

Poverty is closely associated with unemployment in rural areas. In the growth literature of the seventies, two basic assertions have been made. First, there is no substantial evidence with us that the growth of agriculture has sufficiently increased employment in the rural areas. Secondly, the growth in agriculture has not led to an improvement in the standard of living of disadvantaged sections of the society.[10] Recently, a number of programmes viz. IRD programme, National Rural Employment Programmes (NREP) and Rural Landless

Employment Guarantee Programme (RLEGP) have been started in rural areas for weaker sections to provide them minimum needs and productive employment. IRDP helps in providing self-employment to weaker sections by transferring them income generating assets, whereas NREP and RLEGP are meant mainly for providing wage employment to unemployed and/or under-employed persons in rural areas through public sector schemes.

This section investigates the impact of different schemes adopted under IRDP by the selected beneficiaries in Punjab on employment. The main approach of increasing employment of beneficiaries under IRDP is to provide them assets for self-employment. The most popular scheme with the target group is dairying and other animal husbandry enterprises. An attempt is made to discuss how far assets provided under the assistance of the programme has helped in increasing employment of labour for beneficiaries in study area.

Pattern of Labour Use

Table 5.20 shows the labour use per household in different categories of households. It is observed that the major parts of the labour use of beneficiary landless households is devoted to wage paid employment for agricultural work, i.e., 302 mandays per annum per household. Only 73 mandays are utilised for non-agricultural jobs. The persual of Table 5.20 shows that 16.86 per cent of the 451 mandays generated from all activities per year per landless household is used for the various operations of the assets taken on loan and subsidy from the bank under IRDP. Milch-cattle, widely sponsored asset in the study area, is labour intensive. Landless families are engaged in various activities of dairying such as grazing, watering, milking the animal etc.

Marginal and small farmers utilise major portion of their family labour for crop raising. They also use a small amount of casual labour for this purpose. The employment of family labour days has increased with the adoption of employment generating scheme under IRDP. It is observed that 42.44 per cent of the total family labour days, i.e., 87 mandays is generated by the employment generating assets. Labour days devoted to the asset in case of small farmers is only 10.11 per cent of the total family labour used. It is mainly because of the fact that small farmers secured finance for tube-well which is less labour intensive.

TABLE 5.20: Labour Use According to Different Categories of the Sample Households
(*Mandays Per Household*)

Category	Labour employment In			
	Agriculture wage earning/ crop raising	Non-Agri-culture	Employ-ment genera-ted by IRDP scheme	Total
Beneficiary				
1 Landless	302	73	76	451
2. Marginal Farmers				
Family Labour	118	—	87	205
Casual Labour	36	—	—	36
3. Small Farmers				
Family Labour	231	—	26	257
Casual Labour	98	—	—	98
Total				
Landholder				
Family Labour	349	—	113	462
Casual labour	134	—	—	134
Landless	302	73	76	451
Non -Beneficiary				
1 Landless	276	30	20	326
2. Marginal Farmers				
Family Labour	93	—	32	125
Casual Labour	23	—	—	23
3. Small Farmers				
Family Labour	192	—	30	222
Casual Labour	100	—	—	100
TotaL				
Landholder				
Family Labour	285	—	62	347
Casual labour	123	—	—	123
Landless	276	30	20	326

The pattern of labour use on non-beneficiary households is also the same. The number of mandays used by different categories of non-beneficiary households is lower than the same categories of beneficiary households. Apart from other reasons, self-employment generated through the sponsored assets under the IRDP is a crucial factor.

Employment of Landless Labourers

Table 5.21 indicates the position of employment of beneficiary and non-beneficiary landless households. On an average, beneficiary landless households are employed for 451 mandays in a year, whereas non-beneficiaries get employment for only 326 mandays. The employment of labourers is for more days on beneficiary than non-beneficiary households in all the districts. The employment per household is much larger in Malout block of Faridkot district than those of other districts. It may be due to the fact that the cotton crop in the district absorbs less mechanisation, particularly, the picking up of cotton operation where both casual and family labourer are required in large number. In other districts, mechanisation of paddy crop (a major crop there) decreases the use of labour days.

TABLE 5.21: Labour Use Pattern of Landless Labourers

(Mandays Per Household)

Block	Labour use per household			Total
	Wage paid agricultural labour	Wage-paid Non-agricultural labour	Dairying & other animal husbandry activities	
Beneficiary				
Malout	331	93	78	492
Sudhar	295	69	83	447
Batala	278	43	56	377
Overall	302	73	76	451
Non -Beneficiary				
Malout	321	40	20	381
Sudhar	264	30	18	312
Batala	214	8	25	246
Overall	276	30	20	326

Main portion of the total labour days is employed on wage paid agricultural labour in both non-beneficiary and beneficiary landless households. This points to the fact that it is farming which provides them major share of total employment. Besides farming, wage paid non-agricultural employment for non-beneficiary and employment generated through IRDP scheme for beneficiary landless households are also important.

Increase in Labour Use Due to Adoption of IRDP Scheme

The IRD programme has brought a change in the family labour employment of landless households. Table 5.22 shows that on an average an increase of 17 per cent of total mandays has been reported by the beneficiaries of the programme. The main benefit in terms of additional employment under IRDP scheme is to the landless households of Ludhiana district. In this district the dairying activity is progressive due to the existence of a milk plant near Ludhiana.

TABLE 5.22: Changes in Labour Use of Landless Labourers After Adopting the IRDP Scheme

(Mandays Per Household)

Area	Labour Use Per Household		Total
	Labour use without scheme	Employment generated by IRDP scheme	
Faridkot	414 (84.15)	78 (16.85)	492 (100)
Ludhiana	364 (81.43)	83 (18.57)	447 (100)
Gurdaspur	321 (85.16)	56 (14.84)	377 (100)
Total	375 (83.14)	76 (16.86)	451 (100)

Note: Figures in parentheses are percentages

Month-wise Labour Use Pattern of Landless

Table 5.23 shows the pattern of landless labour employment on beneficiary and non-beneficiary households. There is no significant difference in the labour use pattern on the beneficiary and non-beneficiary landless labour households. The intensity of labour use during lean and peak months for beneficiary and non-beneficiary households is the same. Most of the labour days of a household are used in the months of October, November, April, May and June. It is observed that the extent of labour use is higher on beneficiary than on non-beneficiary landless households. Though the assistance under

IRDP has helped in increasing the employment of the beneficiaries yet it has not increased sufficient employment for target group families in the lean months. Therefore, it is not wrong to conclude that the impact of the programme is marginal for landless. The results presented in the Table 5.23 show that farm labour remains under-employed for almost 6 months of a year. This may be one of the most important reasons of poverty of this class.

Table 5.23: Human Labour Use Pattern on Beneficiary and Non-Beneficiary Landless Households

(Mandays Per Household)

Months	Beneficiary			Non-beneficiary
	Agril. & non-agril. labour use	Labour use for IRDP scheme	Total	Agricultural and Non-agricultural labour use
July	16	7	23 (5.10)	18 (5.52)
August	16	6	22 (4.88)	18 (5.52)
September	30	7	37 (8.20)	28 (8.59)
October	51	6	57 (12.64)	42 (12.88)
November	44	6	50 (11.08)	33 (10.12)
December	20	6	26 (5.76)	20 (6.13)
January	26	6	32 (7.10)	24 (7.36)
February	18	7	25 (5.54)	17 (5.21)
March	19	7	26 (5.99)	16 (4.91)
April	48	6	54 (11.97)	34 (11.90)
May	50	6	56 (12.42)	40 (12.27)
June	37	6	43 (9.53)	36 (11.04)
Total	375	76	451 (100)	326 (100)

Note: Figures in parentheses are percentages.

Figures 5.8 and 5.9 reveal that there are two peaks in labour requirement in Punjab. The first peak occurs in the month of October when *Kharif* Crops are harvested followed by ploughing and land preparation for *Rabi*. The second peak occurs in May, the harvest time for *Rabi* crops and sowing time for *Kharif* crops. The labour use in April and November is also good. The labour use for intermediate operation between sowing and harvesting is in other months of the year.

In Fig. 5.8 monthly labour use pattern of beneficiary households without and with scheme has been plotted. It is observed that IRDP scheme has increased the family labour use of the beneficiaries but there is no shift in the peaks.

In Fig. 5.9 monthly labour use pattern of both beneficiary and non-beneficiary households has been plotted. The family labour use is much higher on beneficiary households than non-beneficiary households.

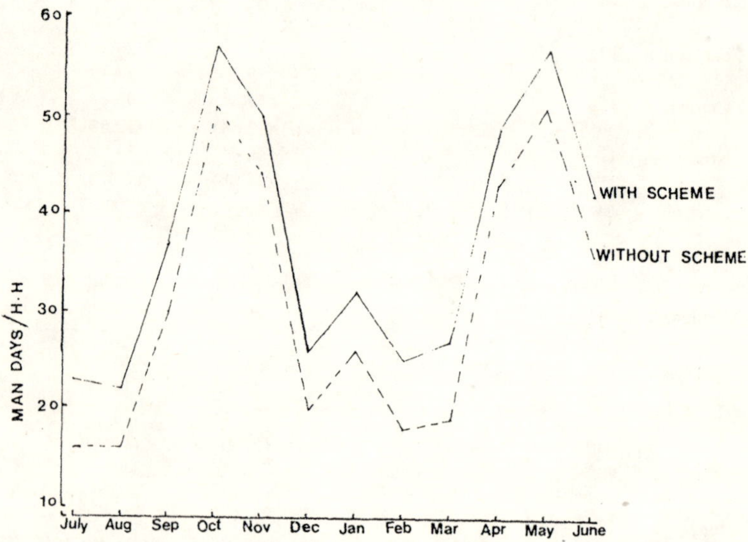

FIG. 5.8: Human Labour use per Household — Without/With Scheme.

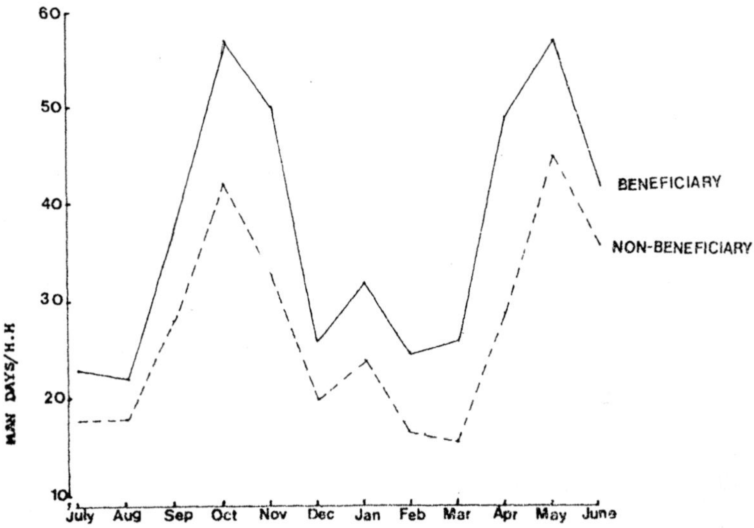

FIG. 5.9: Human Labour use per Household — Landless.

Employment on Landowner Households

The human labour employment on beneficiary and non-beneficiary marginal and small farmers is presented in Table 5.24.

There is little difference in the labour days used per household between beneficiary and non-beneficiary marginal and small farmers. Per acre use of labour on beneficiary marginal farmers is higher than on beneficiary small farmers by 21 per cent.

The perusal of Table 5.24 shows that family labour is a major constituent of total labour for different agricultural operation of different categories of farmers. Casual labour is needed at the time of sowing, harvesting and picking up cotton. Casual labour is used by all the categories of farmers in varying degree.

Increase in Employment on Landless Households due to IRDP

It is observed that the asset provided under IRDP has added to the family labour employment. Table 5.25 shows increase in family labour employment per household of beneficiary farmers. The average employment of family labour per household has improved on both marginal and small farm households after the adoption of the programme. Average increase in employment is 42.44 and 10.11 per cent on marginal and small landowner households, respectively in the study area. The substantial increase of employment of labour on marginal farmers is mainly due to the dairying schemes sponsored under IRDP. These schemes are of self-employment type, therefore, they utilise more family labour. The less increase in labour days on small beneficiary farmers is because of the nature of assets they purchased under the programme. Most of the small farmers in the study area have installed tube-wells which utilise less labour to keep them up.

TABLE 5.24: Labour Use Per Acre of Beneficiaries and Non-Beneficiaries Households of Marginal and Small Farmers for Crop Enterprises

(Mandays)

Area/Category	Marginal						Small					
	Beneficiary			Non-Beneficiary			Beneficiary			Non-Beneficiary		
	F	C	T	F	C	T	F	C	T	F	C	T
Faridkot (Malout Block)	21	10	31	26	7	33	20	7	27	13	14	27
Ludhiana (Sudhar Block)	46	13	59	38	8	46	34	19	53	40	18	58
Gurdaspur (Batala Block)	47	9	46	37	12	49	29	9	38	34	13	47
Overall	38	10	48	33	9	42	27	11	38	20	15	35

F = Family labour; C = Casual Labour; T = Total Labour (F+C)

The highest increase of labour is recorded in case of marginal farmers of Batala block. It is mainly due to the fact that the village Nathwal is close to Batala city. This village along with others fulfils the milk demand of the city people. Therefore, villagers with milch cattle in the village do not face any demand problem. The marginal farmers are running dairying enterprises more successfully since each one has a small field to grow fodder, an important input for dairying. That is why some of the marginal farmers have sought assistance for two buffaloes in this village.

TABLE 5.25: Increase in Family Labour Employment Per Landowner Beneficiary Household

Mandays

Category	Family labour employment in other than IRDP scheme		Employment generated through IRDP scheme		Total		Per cent Increase due to IRDP scheme	
	M	S	M	S	M	S	M	S
1	2	3	4	5	6	7	8	9
Faridkot	90	136	67	24	157	160	42.67	15.00
Ludhiana	161	296	78	31	239	327	32.63	9.48
Gurdaspur	103	261	144	20	273	281	52.74	7.12
Overall	118	231	87	26	205	257	42.44	10.11

M = Marginal Farmers; S = Small Farmers

NOTES

1. A survey of poor families was conducted in September 1980 in Punjab by Punjab Government to identify households below the income of Rs.3,600 per annum. These families were given yellow-cards for identification.
2. B.A. Atkinson, 'On the Measurement of Inequality', *Journal of Economic Theory*, 256-57, February 1970.
3. In this study, special adjustment was made to the figure of income per household of Rs.3,600 per annum to price changes. It was found that those households earning approximately Rs.4,500 per annum or less in the assessment year were below poverty line or termed as target household.
4. Non-effective beneficiaries are those who have either sold the asset acquired under IRDP or it is missing with the beneficiary at the time of survey.
5. (a) Evaluation cell of PNB found in a study (1984) of two districts, Basti and Dehradun, of U.P that almost 19 per cent of the beneficiaries are ineligible for assistance under IRDP and did not constitute part of the target group.
   "An Evaluation Study on IRDP in U.P." Evaluation Cell, PNB, 1984, New Delhi.

   (b) The NABARD (1984) survey pointed towards the fact that the wrong identification was to be 35 per cent in Punjab, 42 per cent in Assam, 18 per cent in Haryana, 19 per cent in M.P. and 13 per cent in Maharashtra.
   NABARD (1984), *Study of Implementation of IRD*, 1984-85, New Delhi.

   (c) Programme Evaluation Organisation of Planning Commission (1985) conducted an evaluation study concluded that about 26 per cent of the 1170 selected beneficiaries were not correctly identified.

PEO, Planning Commission, Evaluation Report on IRDP, 1985 Govt. of India, New Delhi.

6. (a) A survey (1981) conducted by Kerala Planning Board showed that on the basis of annual income about 23 per cent, and on the basis of PCI about 19 per cent beneficiary households have not been properly identified.
State Planning Board, Evaluation Cell, Kerala (1981).
   (b) A case study (1984) conducted by Kutty Krishnan showed that on total household income basis only 20 per cent and on PCI basis 3.6 per cent were poor who deserved assistance under IRDP.
A.C. Kutty Krishnan (1984) : *op. cit.*
7. (a) PEO in its study concluded that 49.42 per cent of the beneficiaries had crossed the poverty line.
PEO, Planning Commission (1985) : *op. cit.*
   (b) The NABARD study showed that the selected districts in States such as Punjab, Haryana, Uttar Pradesh and Maharashtra showed a better performance with more than 40 per cent households rising above poverty line, while Rajasthan, Tamil Nadu and Andhra Pradesh showed 10 per cent or less performance.
NABARD (1984) : *op. cit.*
8. Durable household assets include articles which are expected to give service for fairly long period of time viz., television, radio, electric fans, sewing machine, cycle, furniture and fixture, utensils etc.
9. Livestock includes milch-cattle, draught animal (not shown any where else), goats, sheep and all other farm animals and poultry.
10. (a) D.T. Lakadwala, 'Growth, Unemployment and Poverty', Presidential Address at all India Labour Economics Conference, S.V. Uni., Tripati, December 31, 1977, p. 3.
   (b) G.P. Mishra, 'Development Policy & Planning', *EPW*, May 24, 1969.
   (c) A. Sen, 'Poverty, Inequality and Unemployment', *EPW*, Aug.1973.
   (d) H.S. Bal, 'Impact of Mechanisation on Farm Labour Employment', *ASI*, September, 1974.

SIX

PROBLEMS AND PROSPECTS OF THE PROGRAMME

THE INTEGRATED Rural Development Programme has been in operation in Punjab since 1978. Even this programme has not been able to make a significant dent on either poverty or inequalities or unemployment among a large number of rural people. There may be a number of reasons for the slow progress of the programme. It is, therefore, desirable and imperative to identify some of the selected administrative and other problems of the programme in the study area.

This chapter is based on the informal discussion with block level officials, bank personnels, *panchayat* members, local people and selected beneficiaries and non-beneficiaries of the programme in the study area.

Identification of Target Families and Selection of Beneficiaries

Proper identification is very important factor in the successful implementation of IRD programme. But this remains the least important with the authorities. In Punjab, as reported earlier, a State-wide survey for weaker sections was undertaken in September 1980. All the poor families are provided with a yellow card for identification. These families are selected for the purpose of assistance under the programme. This study and a number of other studies cited somewhere else conclude that the some of the identified and selected poor families are misclassified. In actual practice, a number of underserved families get their names in the list of target families. Though it is difficult to find exactly the deserving poor families in the rural areas yet misclassification can be minimised.

The selected beneficiaries for the purpose of assistance are also not based on *Antyodya* principle. Therefore, it is not ruled out that some of tne influential 'identified' target families might have got the benefits first.

The Government of Punjab has issued instructions to the functionaries of the IRD programme to cancel the yellow cards of those families who cross the minimum level of income for identification. But this is not done so far in the study area.

Most of the bank officials complain against the process of selection of beneficiaries by DRDA and block office. They feel that the programme has been imposed upon them. They show their helplessness that, in the prevailing conditions in the rural Punjab, it is not possible to scrutinise the antecedents of the beneficiaries of the programme.

It is suggested that identification process should be streamlined and updated from time-to-time. Apart from block level officials, bank managers or their representatives, panchayat members and village school teachers may be associated when the survey for identification of target families is being conducted. The survey team should include trained personnels of reputed non-government agency. The final selection of the beneficiary households should be made in the village meeting (Gram Sabha). The poorest of the poor should be chosen first while making a selection for assistance under the programme.

Delay in Assistance to Beneficiaries

It is observed that the submission for application for the scheme to DRDA/block office and the grant of sanction of loan to purchase the asset takes a lot of time. In this sample study, only 20 per cent of the selected beneficiaries could get all the formalities settled within three months. Another 52 per cent beneficiary households received the loan sanctioned between 3 to 9 months. The delay in assistance creates tension in the minds of beneficiaries and thus it gives rise to corrupt practices.

The moment bank officials are approached to ascertain the reasons for delay in sanctioning the applications for the grant of loan to the beneficiaries they complin against the DRDA/block office and inadequate staff in the banks. The loan application are sent to bank by DRDA and block office in a bunch. These get piled up in the end of the financial year, and the bank officials find it difficult to clear them in stipulated time.

The delay in assistance to the beneficiaries, we understand, can be discussed under two headings, block level delay and bank delay. At the block level, the delays are mainly due to time consuming procedure, cross referencing for securing approvals, inefficiency etc. Bank delays may be due to completion of formalities, i.e., paper work, assurance with regard to repayment of loan, inefficiency, inadequate staff support at the bank etc.

The submission of final application for financial assistance by DRDA/block office to the banks should be at the regular intervals. The DRDA and block level office should help bank personnels to fulfil the required formalities for the advance of loans. The authorities should provide sufficient staff to the banks to cope up with the extra work created by IRD programme.

Cumbersome Official Procedure and Corruption

It is veritable true that a large population of the rural poor are illiterate. The investigator finds the same result in the sample study of beneficiaries and non-beneficiaries. The selected target beneficiary families complain against a number of formalities even before applying for loan to block office. They have to go through a number of formalities before getting the finance for the asset. This cumbersome official procedure is one of the reasons which checks the non-beneficiaries from applying for benefit schemes provided under IRD programme.

The beneficiaries also reported against the practice of corruption at various stages of grant of sanction for the benefit schemes, such as, clearance of scheme from block office of DRDA, getting a certificate of fitness from the veterinary doctor for animal husbandry schemes, etc. It is observed that 32 per cent beneficiaries give the hush money to grease the palm of officials at various stages.

There should be one window system for granting loans to target families. This will definitely facilitate and coordinate the entire working of development agencies and financial institutions. Therefore, it is imperative for different agencies such as DRDA, block office, technical expert of the assets and financial institutions to work in close cooperation with one another to enable the beneficiaries to find an easy access to them all at one window.

Poor Quality of Milch Animals

It has already been reported that a majority of beneficiaries opt for animal husbandry schemes, particularly, milch animals. In the present study 90 per cent of the total selected beneficiaries who purchased milch-cattle report that the quality of the animal is not worth the price paid for. In Punjab, the cattle are purchased from the local trade fairs. Generally, the animals do not belong to any known breed. Consequently, most of the milch animals have become a liability on the beneficiaries. It is also observed during the course of study that most of the defaulters of the programme have taken milch-cattle as asset from IRD programme.

It is, therefore, desirable that the animals supplied to the beneficiaries under the IRD programme should be of known breed to enable the beneficiaries to make the most of the yield taken from cattle. If cattle is of local poor breed, it will become a burden to the beneficiary who instead of raising himself above poverty line faces an acute economic difficulty. For this the rural development agency should ensure that the animals are purchased from the recognised cattle breeding farms instead of local trade fairs.

Monitoring and Follow-up Action

Mere sanction and disbursement of loan and subsidy will not automatically banish poverty among the target families. It is observed during the study of selected beneficiaries that no bank and block level officials, after providing the assets to beneficiaries, visit to ascertain the quality of the assets and difficulties faced by the beneficiaries[1]. It means that no follow-up action is taken on the old beneficiaries. 'If the objective of IRDP of raising the income of the identified beneficiaries is to be achieved, it is of paramount importance that the scheme undertaken by the beneficiaries should be followed-up on systematic basis upor the stage of completion of the resultant increase in income'.[2]

The DRDA should regularly monitor the physical progress and assessment of the impact of the programme on the beneficiaries. No adequate attention has been paid in this regard. The physical verification of the assets has become necessary in the light of fake purchases and disappearance of the asset. 'This verification should be attempted not only on a sample basis but should be exhaustive, i.e., each and every beneficiary assisted should be contacted and the existence of his income generating asset should be verified. School teachers, panchayat officials, NSS volunteers, students of agricultural colleges, polytechnicals etc. could be employed to do the assets verification after they have been given suitable orientation with regard to the manner in which they have to carry out their task'.[3]

The spot survey has revealed that majority of the beneficiaries have been assisted by the IRDP with the supply of milch-cattle. But the economic condition of the beneficiaries has never been taken into account while handing over the milch-cattle to them. In some of the cases, the survey has brought to the notice of investigator the miserable plight of the poor beneficiaries who do not even possess the means to buy the inputs to feed their milch-cattle. As a result of this sorrowful state, the cattle remain underfed and soon either go dry or the yield of milk fails to add to the income of the beneficiary and the very purpose of the IRDP scheme is defeated. It will, therefore, be not out of place to suggest that the different agencies assisting the beneficiaries should either supply them the necessary quantity of cattlefeed or give them additional financial help to enable them to buy inputs, at least for one full year after the supply of the cattle to the beneficiary.

Even official guidelines suggest that fodder development may be taken up as an infrastructure development programme both on community land or on the land owned by individual beneficiary.[4] This suggestion is not carried out by the concerned officials in the study area.

It is also observed in the study area that no veterinary doctor visits the beneficiary for medical check-up of cattle. Guidelines of IRDP suggests that 'the block plan should be more specific and it should be indicated clearly that a particular veterinary hospital/dispensary or field assistant shall be responsible for providing this (health) cover, including prophylactic preventive measures. A list of beneficiaries to whom milch animals are provided should be supplied to the concerned veterinary dispensary/field assistant and it should be ensured that these officials pay special attention to the milch animals distributed through the IRD programme. The field assistance should also maintain a record of the health status and production performance of milch-cattle supplied to IRDP beneficiaries and a quarterly report on this should be furnished by them to the DRDA and State veterinary/Animal Husbandry Department'.[5] But this practice is not followed in the study area. Similarly, service repair centres (mobile or fixed) may be provided for mechanical inputs purchased under IRDP to marginal and small farmers.

Livestock – A Major Activity with the Beneficiaries

It is found that the major type of income generating asset in the study area is animal husbandry. It has already been stated that 80 per cent of the sample beneficiary opt for animal husbandry schemes, mainly milch animals. It may be due to the fact that the animal husbandry is very much based on agriculture. This activity does not require any formal training to the beneficiaries also. Even the Draft Seventh Five Year Plan (1985-90), Government of India, also noticed that the selection of schemes under the programme has shown overwhelming bias towards animal husbandry, more particularly milch animal. This has given rise to a number of problems such as shortage of milch animals, increase in their price and other inputs, marketing of output etc. This bias has become a weakness of the programme.

There is need to educate the beneficiary regarding the adoption of a proper scheme. The schemes under secondary and tertiary sectors must also be popularised. These schemes are not given due importance so far in the implementation of the programme. These two activities have the potentialities to absorb surplus manpower from the primary sector. However, there is need to acquire new skills for secondary and tertiary sector schemes. The TRYSEM, KVIB, etc. can help the target families in this regard. Sufficient arrangement should be made to supply raw materials and for the marketing of the output of such enterprises.

Marketing of Output

Marketing of output generated through IRDP scheme is a problem in the study area. In many cases the demand aspect of asset is not properly determined while financing the assets and it naturally results into the fall of price of the output. The study of the villages of Faridkot and Gurdaspur reveals that the price of milk went down due to large supply of milk than its demand. This happens due to adoption of a single activity, i.e., dairying, under IRDP. The selected beneficiary households of these villages complained that they were assured that milk chilling plant and marketing support centres would be set up in their villages before financing the scheme, but the assurances probably had remained on the paper till the time of fieldwork.

Lack of adequate marketing support for the various schemes financed under the IRDP has been one of the major constraints in rural development. It is, therefore, desirable that before granting sanction for assets and loan, the marketing aspect of the output produced by the assets should be studied properly. A detailed market plan for the different commodities produced by assets supplied under IRDP may be prepared after studying the local area and nearby areas.

Repayment of Loan

Recovery of loans described the success of the programme. But the recovery position of the loans in the study area is poor. It is observed during the field survey that 45 per cent of the beneficiaries have either repaid no loan instalment or only up to 20 per cent of the total loan amount. Forty per cent of the beneficiaries repay their loans amounting to 20 to 50 per cent of the total amount of loan.

The main reasons for the default of the loan are that: (i) the disappearance of the assets from the possession of the beneficiary; and (ii) the asset is not economically viable, etc. The bank officials complain that DRDA does not help in the recovery of loans from beneficiaries.

The recovery of the loan should be given due importance in the programme. This will encourage financial institutions to advance more and more loans to the poor people. Both, banks and DRDA, should join hands in recovering the loans. If the beneficiary is in trouble due to certain reasons,e.g., due to illness of animal, natural calamities, defect in the mechanical input etc., it should be monitored to the concerned financial institution and DRDA/block office. These institutions should properly help the troubled beneficiary to get him out of the unfavourable situation.

Income and Its Inequalities

It is observed that the impact of IRDP on beneficiaries particularly landless household is marginal. Most of the below poverty line families are still in poverty-stricken even after the adoption of the programme. It is inferred that the dose of assistance provided to some of the beneficiaries is too small to raise them above poverty line. Therefore, there is continuous need to supplement these families with other income generating activities or to strengthen the existing ones. For example, the second dose of providing buffaloes to the existing beneficiaries having milch animal has not been implemented to the latter and spirit of guidelines of IRDP, issued by Ministry of Rural

Reconstruction, Government of India, New Delhi.[6]

The study reveals that there is sufficient evidence to convince us that some of the better-off-families usurp the benefits actually meant for the target families alone. In case this unhealthy practice remains unchecked, it is feared that the programme, instead of doing good to the target families will simply widen the gap of inequalities among rural people and the target families will stand to suffer the most.

NOTES

1. In a concurrent evaluation by the Department of Rural Development, in the Central Ministry of Agriculture, it has been reported that in the case of Assam, Manipur and Punjab, after care had not been provided in case of 80-85 per cent of the beneficiaries.
   A.P. Saxena "Concurrent Evaluation of IRDP", *EPW*, September 26, 1987, p.A-123.
2. Guidelines for IRDP, Letter written to secretary-in-charge, Rural Development in States, dated 30th March, 1982, Government of India, Ministry of Rural Development, Krishi Bhawan, New Delhi.
3. Guidelines for IRDP, Ministry of Rural Development, Government of India, Letter dated 17th July, 1982.
4. Guidelines for IRDP, Ministry of Rural Reconstruction, Letter dated 27th November 1981, New Delhi.
5. *Ibid.*
6. Guidelines for IRDP, Ministry of Rural Reconstruction, Government of India, Letter dated 27th November 1981.

SEVEN

SUMMARY AND CONCLUSION

THE RURAL development programmes are launched in India to alleviate rural poverty among vulnerable sections of the society. The main thrust of the programmes is to directly help the rural poor by way of providing assets and wage-employment and raise them above poverty line. The vulnerable sections of the society consist of landless labourers, small and marginal farmers, rural artisans and scheduled castes. Presently, a bigger programme of rural development, Integrated Rural Development Programme (IRDP), is working in the rural areas for increasing income and generating employment amongst the unprivileged sections of rural society. In addition, it executes various other schemes as are conducive to improving the quality of life in the villages.

The present book attempts to evaluate the impact of IRDP in Punjab. But, before presenting the results, a critical evaluation of the various rural development programmes has been presented to have an insight into the performance of these programmes. The dismal performance of the programmes has been discussed in the Chapter of Differential Rural Scenario. The evaluation of IRDP is based on both macro and micro data collected from Punjab in the year 1985-86.

The study is based on primary and secondary data. The primary data have been collected from the respondents of three districts of Punjab, eg., Gurdaspur, Ludhiana and Faridkot, selected from three zones, distinct from each other. On all 120 households were surveyed.

The secondary data are based on Statistical Abstracts of Punjab, Annual Plans of Punjab and studies conducted by Government officials, researchers and research organisations.

It is veritabe the that poverty, unemployment and inequality are related issues. Solving any one of the problems will have a favourable impact on the others. But, any how, the alleviating of poverty has been remained the serious concern of the planners and policy-makers since the inception of planning in India. A number of programmes such as Community Development Programme, IADP, IAAP, SFDA, MFALA, etc., have been introduced. But the achievements of these programmes in improving the economic welfare of the poor people and reducing the inequalities have been far from satisfactary. The available data from different sources indicate that the incidence of rural poverty and the economic inequalities have not declined significantly from the rural Punjab. It is established that agricultural development programmes accentuated the inequalities in rural areas.

The data on rural poverty in Punjab for different years showed an erratic trend. In the pre-green revolution period particularly during 1960-66, the incidence of poverty increased sharply mainly because of low agricultural output, high rate of inflation and almost stagnant real wage rates. But after 1966-67, agricultural production increased tremendously due to green revolution in the state. This increase in agricultural production reduced the rural poverty. It is seen that the decrease in rural poverty was not as sharp as the increase in agricultural production. It may be due to the poor 'trickle down' of the benefits from the green revolution to the target group of people. This process could be fastened by institutional changes in the rural sector so that even the target people would have received the benefits from the agricultural development.

Economic inequality among the different strata of rural people explains the relative poverty. Most of the views expressed that green revolution had increased the gap between rich and poor. Therefore, the study of inequalities becomes more important in a State which is pioneer of the green revolution. The present study explains the inequalities in the distribution of consumption, land, assets, credit and wage rates. The available evidence shows that the green revolution in Punjab has improved the condition of almost all the expenditure classes in the rural areas, but the share of bottom 30 per cent of population in consumption expenditure was degenerated in 1970-71, but improved in 1983. It may be due to the fact that green revolution accentuated the distribution of consumption expenditure towards privileged rural people. Therefore, the condition of poor people deteriorated in 1970-71. The improvement in the consumption of poor classes in 1983 might be due to poverty alleviation programmes started after 1970s.

There is skewed distribution of land-holdings in Punjab. The results of three agricultural censuses indicated that the proportion of small and marginal farmers increased from 57 per cent in 1970-71 to 61 per cent in 1976-77, but decreased to 39 per cent in 1980-81. But these farmers operated only 15 per cent of total land in the State. Large farmers (4 hectares or more) accounted for 23, 21 and 33 per cent of agricultural population respectively in 1970-71, 1976-77 and 1980-81 and they operated 65, 64 and 67 per cent of the operational land in the same census years, respectively. The total number of peasants significantly decreased in the year 1980-81 as compared to the years 1970-71 and 1976-77. This shows the de-peasantisation in Punjab agriculture, particularly small and marginal farmers.

It is seen that there were inequalities in the distribution of irrigation and credit in rural areas. While the irrigation base of all the farm sizes had increased in the different census years, the percentage increase in irrigation base rose steeply as we move from small farm size to large farm size. Similarly the credit facilities were mainly enjoyed by the large farmers. Available data indicate that of the total credit advanced by both primary agricultural credit societies and commercial banks, a large proportion of term finance was usurped by the borrowers with holdings of above two hectares.

Wage-employment is an important source of livelihood of rural poor people. Therefore, improvement in the real wages will certainly improve their economic conditions. But the data regarding the real wage rates show that the condition of agricultural labourers did not improve much in the period under study. There was a spurt in real wages in the years 1968 to 1970. It was mainly due to the compulsion of increase in demand for labour due to increase in production due to new agricultural technology. But the pressure of increase in demand could not go a long way partly due to rising mechanisation and partly due to inflow of migrant labour from the neighbouring States in the Punjab. The second time rise in wages was noticed after 1984. This rise may be due to the impact of recent wage employment programmes and decline in the inflow of migrant labour due to abnormal situation in Punjab prevailing since 1984. It is also found that with the increase in agricultural production in Punjab the real wages also increased. But, the increase in wages was very small in relation to the increase in agricultural production. It points to the fact that agricultural development favoured more to the cultivating households and landless agricultural labourers remained the weaker section of the rural society.

There are meagre household and productive assets with the weaker sections. The available data show that there was concentration of assets in favour of the cultivator households with asset group of Rs.20,000 and above in 1970-71. The average value of assets per agricultural labour household was only one-eighteenth of the assets of a cultivator household in Punjab. It shows that there was a large divergence in the economic condition of cultivators and agricultural labourers. This also explains the continuous poverty of the agricultural labourers and prosperity of cultivators.

Appraisal of IRDP

In order to improve the lot of unprivileged rural sections effectively, the programmes such as SFDA and MFALA were merged into the Integrated Rural Development Programme (IRDP) in 1980. The introduction of IRDP was a major departure in emphasis, content and coverage of the rural development strategy. It was assumed that neither the project nor the sectoral approach was adequate for the overall development of the rural areas and for the distribution of benefits to the people especially to those belonging to weaker sections. The main objective of IRDP is to raise the income of the poorest families in rural ares above poverty line by giving them income-generating assets and access to credit and other inputs.

The appraisal of IRDP shows that a number of non poor families have received the benefits of the programme. The survey for the identification of the people below poverty line has not been conducted strictly according to the guidelines provided by the Ministry of Rural Development. The involvement of village agencies and banks in the identification is nil. Even the selection of the beneficiaries is not on the basis of *Antyodya* principle.

Block/district plan which record resource inventory and identify the potentialities of development are not being drawn according to the guidelines. The sectoral distribution of assets shows that there is overemphasis of animal husbandry schemes. It has been seen that most of the defaulters of the programme and the beneficiaries whose assets are not intact, have adopted the animal husbandry schemes. Therefore, there is a need for ratification of sectoral distribution of assets schemes.

The study shows that the programme has improved the economic condition of the beneficiaries with which the assets are intact and in good position. About 50 per cent of the beneficiaries are found to cross the poverty line. Even after this percentage of people crossing the poverty line, a sizeable number of people in Punjab are still poor. This shows the inadequacy of the programme.

Results of the Micro Study

We have found that most of the beneficiaries opted animal husbandry schemes for self-employment. Forty per cent of the beneficiaries were defaulters of the programme. The main reasons for the default were:

(i) The disappearance of the assets with the beneficiary;
(ii) the asset was considered to be economically non-viable; and
(iii) the promise made by one of the political parties during their election campaign to erase all the loans up to Rs.5,000.

Income and Its Distribution

The average income of landless and landowner beneficiaries has increased as compared with their non-beneficiaries counterparts. It is also found that scheme income decreased the number of the households from lower ranges of income to higher ranges. There has been a greater shift in income of landless households than those of marginal farmers.

An attempt is also made to gauge income differentials among beneficiaries and non-beneficiaries, landless and landowner households, and income of the beneficiary without and with scheme income. The analysis shows that in spite of so many flaws in the implementation of IRDP as reported by various studies, it is successful in raising the income of the beneficiaries. But the increase in income is not sufficient to push the beneficiary well above the poverty line.

It is found that the income inequality of beneficiary households reduces with the adoption of IRDP compared with non-beneficiaries. But this reduction in income inequality is marginal. It is evident that the income is concentrated amongst better off households among the beneficiaries of the programme. Therefore, there is a need to review the implementation of the programme for making it more successful.

Consumption Expenditure

The pattern of expenditure on various items of consumption of beneficiary and non-beneficiary households is also similar. There exists a marked difference in average value of per capita consumption of different categories of households. As expected the average value of consumption of landowner beneficiaries and non-beneficiaries is much higher than those of the landless households of the different categories.

The analysis of distribution of consumption expenditure among beneficiary and non-beneficiary households reveals that there is no destitute in the rural areas of selected villages, i.e., having per capita consumption expenditure less than Rs.600 per annum. At the same time no beneficiary landless household and marginal farmer has per capita consumption in the expenditure group of Rs.2,400 and above. The concentration of beneficiary landless and landowner households is in per capita consumption expenditure group of Rs.1,080 and Rs.1,500, whereas the concentration of the small farmers is in the group of Rs.1,800 and Rs.2,400.

There exist consumption inequalities among different segments of landowner and landless households. It is found that non-beneficiary landowner households show more even distribution of expenditure than the beneficiary households. But on the other hand, landless beneficiaries represent less inequalities.

Assets and Its Distribution

The average value of assets with and without land asset of the beneficiaries is Rs.54,991 and Rs.9,507, respectively. The same figures for non-beneficiary counterparts are Rs.44,380 and Rs.4,963, respectively.

There is a big gap between the assets of landless and landowner households. This gap is mainly due to the asset, land. There is positive relationship between size of holding and value of assets. The pattern of distribution of assets among the cultivators is dominated by the nature of distribution of land amongst them. The importance of mechanical as well as non-mechanical inputs increases with the size of holding. The average value of assets of the landless beneficiary households is less than Rs.5,500, whereas this value is Rs.1,04,995 for landowner households. The figures for non-beneficiary landless and landowner households are Rs.2,346 and Rs.86,415, respectively.

The analysis of distribution of assets is carried out by two ways, first, land is excluded from the total assets and secondly, by including land. The main tool of analysis is to divide the total assets of beneficiaries and non-beneficiaries in different assets groups. It is observed that economic condition of landowners is much better than the landless even when the land is not included. Investment made under IRDP schemes has improved the asset group of beneficiaries. The analysis for overall sample households shows that the most of the beneficiaries hold assets in the asset group of Rs.2,500 and Rs.5,000, whereas the concentration of non-beneficiaries remains in the first asset group, i.e., up to Rs.2,500.

The inequality in the possession of assets becomes more acute in case of both landless and landowners households when land asset is also included in the total assets. No beneficiary landowner is found having assets less than Rs.15,000, whereas all the landless households possess assets less than this amount. It is observed that 20 per cent of the landowner households falling in the asset group of Rs.15,000 and Rs.65,000 account for only 10 per cent of the total assets, whereas the same per cent of households owning assets of Rs.1.50 lakh and above possess as high as about 33 per cent of the value of total assets.

Employment

Different income and employment generating schemes under IRD programme have increased family labour employment. This improvement in employment is 16.86 per cent for landless households, 27.78 per cent for marginal and 7.2 per cent for small farmers. The low increase in family labour employment in case of small farmers is mainly due to the fact that these farmers secure finance for tube-wells which is less labour intensive.

The number of mandays used by different categories of non-beneficiary households is less than the same categories of beneficiary households.

The intensity of labour use during lean and peak months for beneficiary and non-beneficiary landless households is almost same. Even the inclusion of employment generated by schemes under IRDP could not change the intensity of lean and peak periods. October-November and April to June are the two major peak seasons. Landless labourers are underemployed for atleast six months of the year.

Problems and Issues of the Programme

On the basis of informal and formal discussion with BDOs, bank personnels, *Panchyat* members and sampled beneficiaries, the following main problems regarding IRD programme are highlighted:

(a) There is undue delay in providing assistance to the beneficiaries. This delay is due to various formalities both at block office and bank level;
(b) There is also complain of corruption particularly for clearance of scheme from Rural Development Agency, getting a certificate of fitness from the veterinary doctor etc.;
(c) There is no follow-up action for the old beneficiaries;
(d) It has been found that livestock activity is not only income augmenting scheme for very poor beneficiaries, but it is still a major activity with the beneficiaries. This bias has become a weakness of the programme;
(e) Marketing facilities for the products generated by the assets sponsored by IRDPs are very poor. Therefore, in some of the areas the price of the product has fallen than before; and
(f) Recovery of the loan is poor in Punjab. The defaulters of the programme are in the same State of affairs as they were at the time of sanctioning the loan.

Implications

It is evident from the above study that income generating assets sponsored under IRDP have helped in increasing the income, consumption, employment and assets of beneficiaries. It has also helped in reducing the inequalities in income of the beneficiaries. Anyhow, it is observed that the impact of the various IRDP schemes on income and employment is marginal. A few suggestions are being made on the basis of above observations.

Since District Rural Development Agencies in Punjab did not conduct any fresh households survey to identify target groups for the purpose of Integrated Rural Development Programme, a number of non-poor families received the assistance under the programme. There is a need to streamline the identification of target families. The involvement of village agencies and banks in the process of identification of poor people is necessary. The *Gram Panchayats* should be involved in the selection of beneficiaries as envisaged in the guidelines. The selection of families must be made on *Antyodaya* principle.

Block/district plans which record resource inventory and identify the potentialities of development must be drawn for the successful implementation of the programme. The obstacles in the way of preparation of these plans must be removed by providing necessary infrastructure such as expertise, trained field staff, computerisation etc.

The sectoral distribution of assets must be according to the local resources available in a cluster of villages, skills of beneficiaries, marketing potential of the products generated by assets, etc. It is suggested that projects with the highest backward and forward linkages should be taken up first under the programme. The identification of these projects need a lot of study. There is a need for diversification of activities sponsored by the State and banks. There is a scope for development of agro-based small industries, horticulture, services given by artisans etc.

IRDP is an anti-poverty programme. It has releved a few families out of poverty line as defined by the various plans. But the condition of relative poverty and inequalities could not change much. Therefore, there is a need to revamp inequitous ownership of assets and power structure in the rural areas along with direct attack on poverty. The need for radical changes in land distribution has been overstated by a number of studies. But much has not been done regarding the implementation of land reform laws enacted during 1950s and 1960s. In Punjab, progressive tax on agricultural income and wealth can bring down the economic inequalities. Generally, this tax is avoided by saying that it will not be viable and give rise to complications. Any how, there is need to enforce these taxes. Efforts should be made to ensure access to inputs, markets and productive employment to the weaker sections of the rural society.

There must be a selection of beneficiaries for self-employment income augmenting schemes. Those poor people who have acquired skills must be given the loans and subsidy for purchasing the assets. Rest of the households should be absorbed in wage employment programmes, i.e., NREP, RLEGP etc. These employment programmes and IRDP should be looked upon as sister programmes. But, wage-employment cannot be considered as a permanent solution of alleviating poverty of the beneficiaries. Therefore, there is an urgent need to make the poor people aware of their constraints and potentialities and provide them necessary skills to undertake suitable projects for self-employment.

Very poor beneficiary households who get milch-cattle should be helped with an additional loan for feeding the animal for atleast one year.

Various schemes adopted by the very poor beneficiaries under IRD programme have just relieved them below the poverty line. But the matter does not finish here. Two main lacune have been observed:

(i) the old beneficiaries are left when the credit for the purchase of asset is provided under IRDP; and
(ii) the management aspect of the asset is totally ignored.

It is suggested that Rural Development Agency and the bank must look after the obstacles of old beneficiaries which impede them in increasing the income from the asset. The short-term courses for the management of income generating assets must also be made compulsory for the beneficiaries. There should be a regular supervision of the assets provided with the beneficiaries by the concerned authorities whether the asset is intact with the beneficiaries and in the proper condition. The students and staff of agricultural universities/ college, school teachers, etc., can also be engaged in this purpose.

The time lag in getting the benefits to the beneficiaries must be minimised. This will check the malpractices and corruption. It can only be done by simplifying the loaning procedure. The recovery of IRDP loan should be considered to be important part of the programme. Bank and Rural Development Agency should educate the borrowers regarding recovery procedure. The recovery of the loan instalment can be suspended for the time being in case the beneficiary is finding some financial problems. The studies should be conducted by the experts regarding the default of the beneficiaries of this programme. This will help in increasing the recovery of the loans.

APPENDICES

APPENDIX A

Consumer Expenditure in Rupees Per Person for One Year by Items of Expenditure

(Landless Beneficiary)

Sl. No.	Items	Consumer Expenditure Range(Rs.)					
		600-840	840-1020	1020-1500	1500-1800	1800-2400	All Classes
1.	Cereals	282 (34.64)	260 (26.89)	323 (26.32)	382 (23.33)	425 (22.44)	320 (26.05)
2.	Pulses	45 (5.53)	71 (7.34)	82 (6.68)	131 (8.00)	109 (5.76)	84 (6.84)
3.	Milk & Its Products	94 (11.55)	119 (12.31)	139 (11.24)	164 (10.02)	163 (8.61)	135 (10.99)
4.	Meat, Egg & Fish	–	59 (6.10)	41 (3.34)	43 (2.63)	–	40 (3.26)
5.	Veg. & Fruits	29 (3.56)	42 (4.34)	52 (4.24)	88 (5.38)	112 (5.91)	56 (4.56)
6.	Sugar & Gur	65 (7.99)	71 (7.34)	104 (8.48)	142 (8.67)	230 (12.14)	104 (8.46)
7.	Misc.	24 (2.95)	22 (2.28)	35 (2.85)	38 (2.32)	53 (2.79)	33 (2.69)
All Food Items (1 to 7)		539 (66.21)	644 (66.60)	772 (62.92)	1006 (61.45)	1091 (57.60)	772 (62.87)
8.	Clothing	176 (21.62)	200 (20.68)	250 (20.37)	293 (17.89)	312 (16.47)	242 (19.21)
9.	Fuel & Light	25 ((3.07)	42 (4.34)	48 (3.91)	64 (3.91)	107 (5.65)	49 (3.99)
10.	Durable Goods	–	–	4 (0.33)	–	31 (1.64)	4 (0.33)
11.	Intoxicants	11 (1.35)	8 (0.83)	25 (2.04)	37 (2.26)	7 (0.37)	21 (1.71)
12.	Education	7 (0.86)	3 (0.31)	7 (0.57)	15 (0.92)	18 (0.95)	8 (0.66)
13.	Medicine	18 (2.21)	28 (2.90)	49 (3.99)	53 (3.24)	75 (3.96)	49 (3.99)

Contd.

APPENDIX A *Contd.*

Sl. No.	Items	Consumer Expenditure Range(Rs.)					
		600-840	840-1020	1020-1500	1500-1800	1800-2400	All Classes
14.	Travelling	38 (4.67)	35 (3.62)	36 (2.93)	79 (4.83)	75 (3.96)	43 (3.55)
15.	Social Ceremonies	—	7 (0.72)	36 (2.93)	89 (5.44)	75 (9.24)	40 (3.26)
	All Non-Food Items (8 to 15)	275 (33.79)	323 (33.40)	455 (37.08)	631 (38.55)	802 (42.40)	456 (37.13)
	Total Expenditure	814 (100)	967 (100)	1227 (100)	1637 (100)	1894 (100)	1228 (100)
	No. of H.H.	2 (6.66)	5 (16.67)	16 (53.33)	5 (16.67)	2 (6.66)	30 (100)
	No. of Persons	17 (8.46)	41 (20.40)	107 (53.23)	28 (13.93)	8 (3.98)	201 (100)

Notes: 1. No landless Beneficiary falls in the range of Rs. 0-600 and Rs. 2400 and above.

2. Figures in parentheses are percentages.

APPENDIX B

Consumer Expenditure in Rupees Per Person for One Year by Items of Expenditure

(Beneficiary Marginal Farmers)

Sl. No.	Items	Consumer Expenditure Range(Rs.)					
		600-840	840-1080	1080-1500	1500-1800	1800-2400	All Classes
1.	Cereals	253 (31.98)	293 (28.69)	339 (27.20)	432 (27.48)	480 (23.39)	348 (27.57)
2.	Pulses	53 ((6.70)	73 (7.15)	95 (7.62)	95 (6.04)	100 (4.87)	85 (6.74)
3.	Milk & its Products	82 (10.37)	118 (11.56)	138 (11.08)	216 (13.74)	200 (9.75)	149 (11.85)
4.	Meat, Egg & Fish	12 (1.52)	—	4 (0.32)	—	48 (2.34)	6 (0.48)
5.	Veg. & Fruits	45 (5.69)	48 (4.70)	57 (4.58)	72 (4.58)	60 (2.92)	58 (4.60)
6.	Sugar & Gur	59 (7.46)	93 (9.11)	109 (8.75)	129 (8.21)	144 (7.02)	105 (8.32)
7.	Misc	32 (4.04)	27 (2.64)	42 (3.37)	94 (5.98)	44 (2.14)	41 (3.24)
	All Food Items (1 to 7)	535 (67.64)	652 (63.86)	785 (63.00)	998 (63.49)	1072 (52.24)	792 (62.76)
8.	Clothing	150 (18.96	214 (20.96)	273 (21.91)	372 (23.66)	600 (29.24)	287 (22.74)
9.	Fuel & Light	44 (5.56)	78 (7.64)	82 (6.58)	69 (4.39)	100 (4.87)	72 (5.71)
10.	Durable Goods	59 (7.46)	14 (1.37)	—	—	60 (2.92)	5 (0.40)
11.	Intoxicants	12 (1.52)	—	6 (0.48)	24 (1.53)	60 (2.92)	14 (1.11)
12.	Education	—	—	25 (2.01)	8 (0.51)	60 (2.92)	14 (1.11)
13.	Medicine	18 (2.28)	32 (3.13)	43 (3.45)	50 (3.18)	40 (1.95)	39 (3.09)

Contd.

APPENDIX B *Contd.*

Sl. No.	Items	Consumer Expenditure Range(Rs.)					
		600-840	840-1080	1080-1500	1500-1800	1800-2400	All Classes
14.	Travelling	24 (3.03)	30 (2.94)	32 (2.57)	50 (3.18)	50 (2.92)	39 (3.09)
15.	Social Ceremonies	—	—	—	—	—	—
	All Non food Item (8 to 15)	256 (32.36)	369 (36.14)	461 (37.00)	574 (36.51)	980 (47.76)	470 (37.24)
	Total Expenditure	791 (100)	1021 (100)	1246 (100)	1572 (100)	2052 (100)	1262 (100)
	No. of H.H.	2 (13.33)	2 (13.33)	5 (33.33)	5 (33.67)	1 (6.66)	15 (100)
	No. of person	17 (15.98)	14 (13.16)	33 (31.02)	25 (23.57)	5 (4.70)	94 (100)

Note: Figures in parentheses are percentages.

APPENDIX C

Consumer Expenditure in Rupees Per Person for One Year by Items of Expenditure

(Beneficiary Small Farmers)

Sl. No.	Items	Consumer Expenditure Range(Rs.)					
		600-1080	1080-1500	1500-1800	1800-2400	2400 & Above	All Classes
1.	Cereals	200 (19.06)	279 (21.86)	341 (20.32)	453 (21.53)	489 (19.34)	349 (20.84)
2.	Pulses	74 (7.05)	82 (6.43)	87 (5.18)	121 (5.75)	147 (5.81)	99 (5.91)
3.	Milk & its Products	167 (15.92)	225 (17.63)	250 (14.90)	330 (15.68)	322 (12.73)	276 (16.48)
4.	Meat, Egg & Fish	—	25 (1.96)	67 (3.99)	58 (2.76)	33 (1.31)	40 (2.39)
5.	Veg. & Fruits	41 (3.91)	90 (7.05)	98 (5.84)	134 (6.37)	120 (4.75)	99 (5.91)
6.	Sugar & Gur	94 (8.96)	104 (8.15)	163 (9.71)	175 (8.31)	218 (8.62)	136 (8.12)
7.	Misc.	29 (2.76)	40 (3.13)	36 (2.14)	58 (2.76)	74 (2.93)	56 (3.34)
	All Food Items (1 to 7)	585 (55.77)	844 (66.14)	1042 (62.09)	1330 (63.21)	1624 (64.24)	1046 (62.44)
8.	Clothing	282 (26.88)	196 (15.36)	273 (16.27)	417 (19.82)	367 (14.52)	307 (18.33)
9.	Fuel & Light	29 (5.62)	75 (5.08)	100 (5.96)	120 (5.70)	134 (5.30)	96 (5.73)
10.	Durable Goods	—	—	—	5 (0.24)	17 (0.67)	3 (0.18)
11.	Intoxicants	—	21 (1.65)	11 (2.44)	30 (1.43)	—	23 (1.37)
12.	Education	28 (2.67)	8 (0.63)	73 (4.35)	75 (3.56)	87 (3.44)	53 (3.16)
13.	Medicine	35 (3.34)	67 (5.25)	89 (5.30)	70 (3.33)	122 (4.82)	72 (4.30)

Contd.

APPENDIX C *Contd.*

Sl. No.	Items	Consumer Expenditure Range(Rs.)					
		600-1080	1080-1500	1500-1800	1800-2400	2400 & Above	All Classes
14.	Travelling	59 (5.62)	67 (5.25)	55 (3.27)	73 (3.47)	122 (4.83)	70 (4.18)
15.	Social Ceremonies	—	—	7 (0.41)	—	56 (2.21)	6 (0.36)
	All Non-food Items (8 to 15)	464 (44.23)	432 (33.86)	636 (37.90)	794 (37.74)	904 (35.76)	629 (37.55)
	Total Expenditure	1049 (100)	1276 (100)	1678 (100)	2104 (100)	2528 (100)	1675 (100)
	No. of H.H.	1 (6.67)	3 (20.00)	3 (20.00)	6 (40.00)	2 (13.33)	15 (100)
	No. of Person	17 (16.67)	24 (23.53)	22 (21.57)	30 (29.41)	9 (8.82)	102 (100)

Notes: 1. No consumer is having expenditure less than Rs. 840.
2. Figures in parentheses are percentages.

APPENDIX D

Consumer Expenditure in Rupees Per Person for One Year by Items of Expenditure

(Beneficiary: Overall)

Sl. No.	Items	Consumer Expenditure Range(Rs.)						
		600-840	840-1080	1080-1500	1500-1800	1800-2400	2400 & Above	All Classes
1.	Cereals	268 (33.37)	253 (25.37)	320 (25.84)	387 (23.79)	451 (10.60)	489 (19.34)	334 (24.36)
2.	Pulses	49 (6.10)	72 (7.22)	85 (6.86)	106 (6.51)	116 (5.30)	147 (5.81)	88 (6.42)
3.	Milk & its Products	88 (10.96)	125 (12.53)	141 (11.39)	207 (12.72)	284 (12.97)	322 (12.74)	166 (12.11)
4.	Fish, Egg & Meat	6 (0.75)	33 (3.31)	31 (2.50)	36 (2.21)	46 (2.10)	33 (1.31)	32 (2.33)
5.	Veg. & Fruits	37 (4.61)	43 (4.31)	59 (4.77)	85 (5.22)	122 (5.27)	120 (4.75)	67 (4.89)
6.	Sugar & Gur	62 (7.72)	81 (8.12)	105 (8.48)	144 (8.85)	181 (8.27)	218 (8.62)	115 (8.39)
7.	Misc.	28 (3.49)	25 (2.51)	37 (2.99)	56 (3.44)	56 (2.56)	74 (2.93)	41 (2.99)
	All Food Items (1 to 7)	537 (66.87)	632 (63.39)	785 (63.40)	014 (62.32)	1256 (57.38)	1624 (64.24)	843 (61.48)
8.	Clothing	168 (20.92)	222 (22.27)	247 (19.95)	313 (19.23)	419 (19.14)	367 (14.51)	270 (19.69)
9.	Fuel & Light	34 (4.36)	53 (5.32)	120 (9.69)	76 (4.67)	115 (5.25)	134 (5.30)	92 (6.71)
10.	Durable Goods	—	3 (0.30)	2 (0.16)	—	16 (0.73)	17 (0.67)	3 (0.22)
11.	Intoxicants	11 (1.37)	4 (0.40)	21 (1.70)	34 (2.09)	29 (1.32)	—	20 (1.46)
12.	Education	4 (0.50)	8 (0.80)	11 (0.89)	30 (1.84)	65 (2.97)	87 (3.44)	21 (1.47)
13.	Medicine	18 (2.24)	24 (2.41)	50 (4.04)	63 (3.87)	70 (3.20)	122 (4.83)	49 (3.57)
14.	Travelling	31 (3.86)	40 (4.01)	39 (3.15)	62 (3.81)	74 (3.38)	122 (4.83)	49 (3.57)
15.	Social Ceremonies	—	10 (1.00)	23 (1.86)	35 (2.15)	40 (1.83)	56 (2.22)	24 (1.75)
	All Non-Food Items (8 to 15)	— (33.13)	266 (36.61)	365 (36.59)	453613 (37.68)	815 (37.23)	904 (35.76)	528 (38.52)
	Total Expenditure	803 (100)	997 (100)	1238 (100)	627 100)	2189 (100)	2528 (100)	1371 (100)
	No. of H.H.	4 (6.67)	8 (13.33)	24 (40.00)	13 (21.67)	9 (15.00)	2 (3.33)	60 (100)
	No. of Persons	34 (8.56)	72 (18.14)	164 (41.31)	75 (18.89)	43 (10.82)	9 (2.27)	397 (100)

Note: 1. Figures in parentheses are percentages.

2. There is no consumer having expenditure less than Rs. 600.

APPENDIX E

Consumer Expenditure in Rupees Per Person for One Year by Items of Expenditure

(Landless Non-Beneficiary)

Sl. No.	Items	Consumer Expenditure Range(Rs.)					
		600-840	840-1020	1020-1500	1500-1800	1800-2400	All Classes
1.	Cereals	257 (32.41)	303 (31.82)	401 (30.82)	320 (20.80)	500 (24.38)	340 (31.10)
2.	Pulses	71 (8.95)	67 (7.04)	98 (7.53)	80 (5.02)	160 (7.95)	79 (7.23)
3.	Milk & its Products	86 (10.84)	80 (8.40)	126 (9.68)	140 (8.78)	241 (11.75)	100 (9.15)
4.	Fish, Egg & Meat	—	16 (1.68)	31 (2.38)	—	50 (2.44)	20 (1.83)
5.	Veg. & Fruits	43 (5.42)	36 (3.78)	46 (3.53)	40 (2.51)	142 (6.92)	43 (3.93)
6.	Sugar & Gur	86 (10.84)	88 (9.24)	121 (9.30)	100 (6.27)	200 (9.75)	101 (9.16)
7.	Misc.	21 (2.65)	37 (3.89)	52 (4.00)	34 (2.13)	58 (2.83)	41 (3.75)
	All Food Items (1 to 7)	564 (71.12)	636 (66.81)	876 (67.33)	714 (44.79)	1355 (66.07)	723 (66.14)
8.	Clothing	143 (18.03)	204 (21.43)	218 (16.76)	200 (12.54)	417 (20.33)	213 (19.48)
9.	Fuel & Light	36 (4.54)	39 (4.10)	63 (4.85)	40 (2.51)	77 (3.75)	47 (4.30)
10.	Durable Goods	—	9 (0.95)	11 (0.84)	—	—	9 (0.82)
11.	Intoxicants	—	14 (1.47)	19 (1.46)	40 (2.51)	33 (1.61)	16 (1.46)
12.	Education	—	6 (0.63)	5 (0.38)	100 (6.27)	—	8 (0.73)
13.	Medicine	29 (3.66)	14 (1.47)	32 (2.46)	40 (2.51)	53 (2.58)	24 (2.19)

Contd.

APPENDIX E *Contd.*

Sl. No.	Items	Consumer Expenditure Range(Rs.)					
		600-840	840-1020	1020-1500	1500-1800	1800-2400	All Classes
14.	Travelling	21 (2.65)	20 (2.10)	39 (3.00)	60 (3.76)	84 (4.10)	28 (2.56)
15.	Social Ceremonies	—	5 (0.52)	37 (0.84)	400 (25.09)	33 (1.61)	25 (2.29)
	All Non-Food (8 to 15)	229 (28.88)	316 (13.29)	425 (32.67)	880 (55.20)	697 (33.98)	370 (33.85)
	Total Expenditure	793 (100)	952 (100)	1301 (100)	1591 (100)	2051 (100)	1093 (10C)
	No. of H.H.	1 (3.33)	16 (53.33)	10 (33.34)	1 (3.33)	2 (6.67)	30 (100)
	No. of persons	7 (3.83)	116 (63.39)	49 (26.78)	5 (2.73)	6 (3.28)	183 (100)

Notes: 1. Figures in parentheses are percentages.
2. No consumer falls in expenditure parentheses of Rs. 0-600 and Rs. 2400 and above.

APPENDIX F

Consumer Expenditure in Rupees Per Person for One Year by Items of Expenditure

(Marginal Non-Beneficiary)

Sl. No.	Items	Consumer Expenditure Range (Rs.)					
		840-1080	1080-1500	1500-1800	1800-2400	2400 & Above	All Classes
1.	Cereals	350	358	448	515	600	520
		(33.46)	(25.72)	(27.28)	(25.21)	(23.44)	(30.90)
2.	Pulses	60	61	103	123	225	100
		(5.74)	(4.38	(6.27)	(6.02)	(8.79)	(5.94)
3.	Milk & its Products	9	163	160	281	300	197
		(8.60)	(11.71)	(9.74)	(13.75)	(11.72)	(11.71)
4.	Fish, Egg & Meat	40	26	28	23	—	26
		(3.82)	(1.87)	(1.70)	(1.12)		(1.54)
5.	Veg. & Fruits	30	76	87	107	225	91
		(2.87)	(5.46)	(5.30)	(5.24)	(8.79)	(5.41)
6.	Sugar & Gur	80	105	140	183	250	144
		(7.64)	(7.54)	(8.53)	(8.96)	(9.77)	(8.56)
7.	Misc.	20	50	58	61	125	56
		(1.91)	(3.59	(3.53)	(2.99)	(4.88)	(3.32)
	All Food Items (1 to 7)	620	839	1023	1294	1725	1051
		(59.27)	(60.27)	(62.30)	(63.34)	(67.38)	(62.45)
8.	Clothing	300	276	409	400	375	360
		(28.68)	(19.83)	(24.91)	(19.58)	(14.64)	(21.39)
9.	Fuel & Light	40	63	87	127	160	17
		(3.82)	(4.53)	(5.30)	(6.22)	(6.25)	(1.01)
10.	Durable Goods	—	26	—	11	—	6
			(1.87)		(0.54)		(0.36)
11.	Intoxicants	30	8	13	8	—	16
		(2.87)	(0.57)	(0.79)	(0.39)		(0.95)
12.	Education	—	71	21	35	—	19
			(5.10)	(1.28)	(1.71)		(1.13)
13.	Medicine	36	71	56	92	150	73
		(3.44)	(5.10)	(3.41)	(4.50)	(5.86)	(4.39)

Contd.

APPENDIX F *Contd.*

Sl. No.	Items	Consumer Expenditure Range (Rs.)					
		840-1080	1080-1500	1500-1800	1800-2400	2400 & Above	All Classes
14.	Travelling	20 (1.91)	68 (4.88)	33 (2.01)	77 (3.77)	150 (5.86)	59 (3.50)
15.	Social Ceremonies	—	26 (1.27)	—	—	—	6 (0.30)
	All Non-food Items (8 to 15)	426 (40.73)	553 (39.73)	619 (37.70)	749 (36.66)	835 (32.62)	632 (32.15)
	Total Expen-diture 1 to 15	1046 (100)	1392 (100)	1642 (100)	2043 (100)	2560 (100)	1683 (100)
	No. of H.H.	1 (6.67)	3 (20.00)	4. (26.67)	6 (40.00)	1 (6.66)	15 (100)
	No. of persons	10 (12.20)	19 (23.17)	23 (28.05)	26 (31.71)	4 (14.87)	82 (100)

Notes: 1. Figures in parentheses are percentages.
2. No Consumer is having expenditure less than Rs. 840.

APPENDIX G

Consumer Expenditure in Rupees Per Person for One Year by Items of Expenditure

(Small Non-Beneficiary)

Sl. No.	Items	Consumer Expenditure Range (Rs.)				
		1080-1500	1500-1800	1800-2400	2400-& Above	All Classes
1.	Cereals	355 (29.49)	422 (24.81)	576 (28.21)	750 (25.41)	433 (26.67)
2.	Pulses	81 (6.73)	73 (4.29)	110 (5.38)	75 (2.54)	88 (5.42)
3.	Milk & its Products	118 (9.80)	194 (11.40)	258 (12.64)	500 (16.94)	190 (11.71)
4.	Meat, Egg & Fish	10 (8.83)	22 (1.29)	22 (1.08)	135 (4.57)	21 (1.29)
5.	Veg. & Fruits	61 (5.00)	102 (6.00)	90 (4.40)	112 (3.79)	79 (4.87)
6.	Sugar & Gur	87 (7.23)	110 (6.47)	180 (8.81)	325 (11.01)	130 (8.01)
7.	Misc	36 (2.99)	38 (2.23)	82 (4.02)	140 (4.74)	55 (3.39)
	All Food Items (1 to 7)	748 (62.13)	962 (56.55)	1258 (61.60)	2037 (69.00)	996 (61.37)
8.	Clothing	236 (19.60)	333 (19.58)	329 (16.11)	500 (16.94)	293 (18.05)
9.	Fuel & Light	99 (8.22)	133 (7.82)	90 (4.41)	90 (3.05)	102 (6.28)
10.	Durable Good	11 (0.91)	—	—	—	5 (0.31)
11.	Intoxicants	—	117 (6.88)	81 (3.97)	100 (3.39)	50 (3.08)
12.	Education	32 (2.66)	17 (1.00)	39 (1.91)	—	30 (1.85)
13.	Medicine	47 (3.90)	64 (3.76)	119 (5.83)	100 (3.38)	75 (4.62)

Contd.

APPENDIX G *Contd.*

Sl. No.	Items	Consumer Expenditure Range (Rs.)				
		1080-1500	1500-1800	1800-2400	2400- & Above	All Classes
14.	Travelling	32 (2.65)	67 (3.94)	126 (6.17)	125 (4.23)	71 (4.37)
15.	Social Ceremonies	—	8 (0.47)	—	—	2 (0.12)
	All Non-Food Items (8 to 15)	456 (32.87)	739 (43.44)	784 (38.40)	915 (31.00)	627 (38.62)
	Total Expenditure	1204 (100)	1701 (100)	2042 (100)	2952 (100)	1623 (100)
	No. of H.H.	6 (40.00)	3 (20.00)	5 (33.33)	1 (6.67)	15 (100)
	No. of Persons	47 (47.00)	18 (18.00)	31 (31.00)	4 (4.00)	100 (100)

Notes: 1. There is no consumer in Expenditure Ranges of less than Rs. 1080
2. Figures in parentheses are percentages.

APPENDIX II

Consumer Expenditure in Rupees Per Person for One Year by Items of Expenditure

(Overall Non-Beneficiary)

Sl. No.	Items	Consumer Expenditure Range (Rs.)						
		600-840	840-1080 1500	1080- 1800	1500- 2400	1800- Above	2400 & Classes	All
1.	Cereals	257 (32.41)	307 (32.01)	375 (29.37)	424 (25.54)	514 (25.16)	675 (24.49)	430 (31.36)
2.	Pulses	71 (8.95)	66 (6.88)	85 (6.66)	89 (5.36)	121 (5.92)	150 (5.44)	86 (6.27)
3.	Milk & Its Products	86 (10.84)	81 (8.45)	129 (10.10)	171 (10.30)	226 (13.02)	400 (14.51)	146 (10.65)
4.	Meat, Egg & Fish	—	17 (1.77)	22 (1.72)	22 (1.33)	25 (1.22)	67 (2.43)	22 (1.60)
5.	Veg. & Fruits	43 (5.42)	36 (3.75)	57 (4.46)	88 (5.30)	102 (4.99)	169 (6.13)	64 (4.67)
6.	Sugar & Gur	86 (10.84)	87 (9.07)	105 (8.22)	124 (7.47)	183 (8.96)	288 (10.45)	118 (8.61)
7.	Misc.	21 (2.65)	35 (3.65)	45 (3.52)	48 (2.89)	71 (3.47)	132 (4.79)	48 (3.50)
	All Food Items (1 to 7)	564 (71.12)	634 (66.11)	818 (64.05)	966 (58.19)	1282 (62.75)	1881 (68.25)	872 (63.60)
8.	Clothing	143 (18.03)	212 (22.11)	235 (18.40)	357 (21.51)	367 (17.96)	437 (15.86)	268 (19.55)
9.	Fuel & Light	36 (4.54)	39 (4.07)	77 (6.03)	100 (6.02)	104 (5.09)	125 (4.54)	72 (5.72)
10.	Durable Goods	—	8 (0.83)	11 (0.86)	—	4 (0.20)	—	7 (0.51)
11.	Intoxicants	—	15 (1.56)	12 (0.94)	57 (3.43)	46 (2.25)	50 (1.81)	25 (1.82)
12.	Education	—	6 (0.63)	16 (1.25)	28 (1.69)	33 (1.62)	—	16 (1.17)
13.	Medicine	29 (3.66)	16 (1.67)	45 (3.52)	58 (3.49)	102 (4.99)	125 (4.54)	48 (3.50)
14.	Travelling	21 (2.65)	20 (2.09)	41 (3.21)	107 (6.45)	102 (4.99)	137 (4.97)	47 (3.49)
15.	Social Ceremonies	—	8 (0.83)	20 (1.57)	47 (2.83)	3 (0.15)	—	14 (1.02)
	All Non-Food Item (8 to 15)	229 (28.88)	325 (23.84)	450 (35.95)	695 (41.81)	761 (37.24)	875 (31.75)	498 (36.40)
	Total Expenditure	793 (100)	959 (100)	1277 (100)	1660 (100)	2043 (100)	2756 (100)	1370 (100)
	No. of H.H.	1 (1.67)	17 (28.33)	19 (31.67)	8 (13.33)	13 (21.67)	2 (3.33)	60 (100)
	No. of Persons	7 (1.92)	126 (34.52)	115 (31.51)	46 (12.60)	63 (17.26)	8 (2.19)	365 (100)

Notes: 1. Figure in parentheses are percentages.

2. There is no consumer having expenditure less than Rs. 600.

BIBLIOGRAPHY

Ahluwalia, M.S., 'Rural Poverty and Agricultural Performance in India', *Journal of Development Studies*, April 1978.

———, 'Rural Poverty in India; 1956-57 to 1973-74', World Bank Staff Working Paper No. 279, P. 11.

Alexander, K.C., and Naidu, N.Y., 'Flow of credit and subsidy under IRDP: A study across five States: Madhya Pradesh', *Journal of Rural Development*, 3(5), September 1984.

Arora, D.R. 'Employment generation in rural Punjab through flaying centres', *Khadi-Gramodyog*, April 1981.

Balkrishna, S., 'Monitoring of IRDP', *Journal of Rural Development*, May 1985.

———, 'Management information systems for IRDP', *Yojana*, December 1983.

Baldev Singh & Vinod Kumar, 'Impact of technological change on farm employment', *Indian Journal of Labour Economics*. October 1982.

Bandyopadhyaya, J., *The Poverty of Nations*, New Delhi: Allied Publishers Pvt. Ltd., 1988.

Bardhan, P.K., 'Poverty and 'Trickle Down' in Rural India: A Quantitative Analysis', in Mellor and Desai (ed.), *Agricultural Change and Rural Poverty*, Delhi: Oxford University Press, 1986.

———, 'On the Incidence of Poverty in Rural India of the Sixties', *EPW*, February 1973.

———, 'Inequality in farm Incomes', *EPW*, 1974.

Batra, J.D., 'Integrated rural Uplifts in Punjab', *Kurukshetra*, April 1978.

Bhalla, G.S. and G.K. Chadha, *Green Revolution and the Small Peasants: A study of Income Distribution among Punjab Cultivators*, New Delhi: Concept Publishing Co., 1983.

Bhalla Sheila, 'Real Wage Rates of Agricultural Labourers in Punjab, 1961-77. A Preliminary Analysis', *EPW* 30 June, 1979.

Bhatia, B.S., 'Rural development: A case study of integrated rural development project in Punjab', *Indian Journal of Commerce*, June 1979.

Braham Prakash, 'Planning for rural development: Evaluation of the 1978-83 plants', *Productivity*, Jan.-March 1979.

Chadha, G.K., *The State and Rural Economic Transformation*', New Delhi: Sage Publications, 1986.

Chandhoke, S.K., *Nature and Structure of Rural Habitation*, New Delhi: Concept Publishing Company, 1990.

Chavan, S.B., 'Integrated rural development in national economy', *Khadi-Gramodyog*, October 1981.

Dak, T.M., *Social Inequalities and Rural Development*, New Delhi: National Publishing House, 1962.

Danda, A.K., (ed)., *Studies in Rural Development: Experiences and Issues*, New Delhi: Inter-India Publications, 1984.

Dandekar, V.M. & N. Rath. *Poverty in India*, Bombay: Indian School of Political Economy, 1971.

Desai, G.M., 'Trends in Rural Poverty in India: An Interpretation of Dharam Narain', in Mellor and Desai (ed.), *Agricultural Change and Rural Poverty*, Delhi: Oxford University Press, 1986.

Desai, Vasant, *Rural Development*, Vols. 1 to 5, Bombay: Himalaya Publishing House, 1988.

Desh, B.P., 'Planning Strategy for the Rural Poor: Some leading issues'. *VISION*, Vol. IV, Oct., Dec. 1984.

Frankel, F.R., *India's Green Revolution: Economic Gains and Political Costs*, Princeton: Princeton University Press, 1971.

Gill, Sucha Singh, 'Impact of Economic Development on Rural Artisans in Punjab', *Indian Journal of Labour Economics*, October, 1980.

Giriappe Somu, *Income, Saving and Investment Pattern in Rural India*, New Delhi: Ashish Publication House, 1985.

Govt. of India, The NSS 17th Round (September 1961 - July 1962), No. 144, Tables with Notes on Some Aspects of Landholdings in Rural Areas, New Delhi, 1970.

———, Various issues of *Sarvekshna*.

———, *Manual of IRDP*, Ministry of Rural Reconstruction, New Delhi, 1980.

———, *Instructions for Implementation of RLEGP*, Ministry of Agriculture and Rural Development, New Delhi, 1985.

———, *National Rural Employment Programme, Guidelines*, Ministry of Agriculture and Rural Development, New Delhi, 1985.

———, *Annual Report, 1985-86*, Ministry of Agriculture and Rural Development, New Delhi, 1986.

———, *Evaluation Study Report on IRDP for 1983-84*, The Programme Evaluation Organisation, New Delhi, Planning Commission, 1984.

———, *Draft Seventh Five Year Plan (1985-90)*, New Delhi, Planning Commission.

———, *Concurrent Evaluation of IRDP*, Feb. 1987.

Govt. of Punjab, *Statistical Abstract of Punjab for various years*, Chandigarh, ESO.

———, *Annual Plans for the various years.*

———, Farm Accounts in Punjab, ESO.

———, Identification of Weaker Sections in Punjab, Publication No. 362, Chandigarh, ESO, 1981.

———, *Report of Agricultural Census, 1980-81*, Chandigarh, Department of Agriculture, 1985.

———, Integrated Rural Development Programme (An Evaluation), Publication No. 544, 1987.

———, *Sixth Five Year Plan, 1980-85*, Chandigarh, ESO.

———, *IRDP in Punjab, Project Report for 1977-78 to 1981-82*, Chandigarh.

Gupta, Malay, 'Planning for Rural Development – The IRDP & its strategy: Case Study', *IJAE*, July-Sep. 1984.

Haque, T and S. Verma, 'Regional and Class Disparities in the Flow of Agricultural Credit', *IJAE*, Vol. 43, July-Sep. 1988.

Jain, L.C., *Grass Without Roots: Rural Development under Govt. Auspices*, Research Project Sponsored by ICSSR, 1984.

Jaiswal, N.P., 'Role of Self-Employment in IRD Programmes', *Khadi-Gramodyog*, 28(1), Oct., 1981.

Johl, S.S., *Future of Agriculture in Punjab*, Centre for Research in Rural and Industrial Development, Chandigarh, 1988.

Jose, A.V., 'Trends in Real Wage Rates of Agricultural Labour', *EPW*, 1971.

Kahlon A.S. *et al.*, The Dynamics of Punjab Agriculture, Ludhiana: Punjab Agricultural University, 1972.

———, 'Impact of mechanisation on Punjab Agriculture with Special Reference to Tractorisation', *IJAE*, October-December, 1976.

Kanta, A. and Pardeep Bhargava, *IRDP: An Evaluation of Jaipur District*, Jaipur, Institute of Development Studies, 1984.

Krishnan, A.C. Kutty , 'A case study of IRDP in a Kerala Village', *IJAE*, July - September, 1985.

Krishna, Raj, 'The Crucial Phase of Rural Development', *Kurukshetra*, Nov. 1, 1979.

Kurien, C.T., *Dynamics of Rural Transformation: A Case study of Tamil Nadu, 1950-75*, Delhi: Orient Longman, 1981.

Kurian, N.J., 'IRDP: How Relevant is it?' *EPW*, December 26, 1987.

Lipton, M, 'Inter-farm, Inter-regional and farm and non-farm Income Distribution', *World Development*, Vol. 6, 1978.

Mahajan, R.K., *Impact of Improved Farm Technology on Income, Productivity and Employment*, Ph.D. Thesis, Jammu University, 1980.

———, 'Dynamics of Agriculture and Wages of Agricultural Labourers', *MDU Research Journal (Arts)*, Oct., 1987.

———, 'Aspects of Rural Poverty in Punjab', *Jammu University Research Journal of Social Sciences*, August, 1986.

Malyadri, P., 'Trysem and Self-employment in Rural Areas: The Malady and Remedy', *Rural India*, March 1985.

Mathew, T. (ed.), *Rural Development in India*, New Delhi: Agricole Publishing House, 1984.

Mathur, Hari Mohan, 'Reaching the poor in Rural Areas; Development issues and administrative requirements', *Man and Development*, September, 1984.

Mellor, J.W. and G.M. Desai (ed.), *Agricultural Change and Rural Poverty*, Delhi: Oxford University Press, 1986.

Minhas, B.S., 'Rural Poverty, Land Redistribution and Development', *Indian Economic Review*, April, 1970.

Mishra, G.P., *Dynamics of Rural Development in Village India*, New Delhi: Ashish Publishing House, 1982.

Mishra, R.P. & K.V. Sundharam (ed.), *Rural Area Development – Perspectives and Approaches*, New Delhi: Sterling Publishing Pvt., Ltd., 1979.

Misra, R.P. (ed.) *Rural Development: Capitalist and Social Paths* (5 Vols.), New Delhi: Concept Publishing Company, 1988.

Misra, R.P. and R.N. Achyutha, *Micro-Level Planning: Principles, Methods and Case Studies*, New Delhi: Concept Publishing Company, 1990.

———, *District Planning: A Handbook*,, New Delhi: Concept Publishing Company, 1990.

Misra, V.N., 'Poverty in Rural India; An interregional analysis', *Journal of Social and Economic Studies*, April - June, 1984.

Mua, A. and Chaudhri, D.P. (ed.), *Rural Development and the State*, London, Methuen & Co., Ltd., 1983.

Naidu, I.J., 'Technology for Small Farmers', *Yojna*, June 1, 1977.

NABARD, Study of Implementation of IRDP, Bombay, 1984.

Oberai, A.S., and H.K. Manmohan Singh, 'Migration Flows in Punjab's Green Revolution Belt', *EPW*, March 29, 1980.

———, 'Migration, Remittances and Rural Development, Findings of a Case Study in the Indian Punjab', *International Labour Review*, March-April 1980.

Ooman, M.A., Dynamics of Rural Transformation: A case study of Kerala, A Research Project sponsored by University of Calicut, 1983.

Parthasarathy, G., 'Changes in the Incidence of Rural Poverty and Recent Trends', Presidential Address, Udaipur, 46th Annual Conference of the Indian Society of Agricultural Economics, 1986.

Prasad, Kamta, *Planning for Poverty Alleviation*, New Delhi: Agricole Publishing Academy, 1985.

Prasad, Pradhan H., 'Poverty and Agricultural Development', *EPW*, December 14, 1985.

Punjab National Bank, *An Evaluation Study of IRDP*, New Delhi, Evaluation Cell, 1984.

Rajaraman, I., 'Poverty, Inequality and Economic Growth: Rural Punjab, 1960-61–1970-71' *Journal of Development Studies*, July, 1975.

Rangacharyulu, S.V., 'Beneficiaries meetings: A monitoring mechanism for IRDP', *Journal of Rural Development*, Nov., 1984.

Rao, C.H.H., *Technological change and Distribution of Gains in Indian Agriculture*, New Delhi: Macmillan, 1975.

Rao, V.K.R.V., 'Integrated Rural Development: The Concept,' *Commerce*, August 18, 1979.

Rath, Nilkantha, 'Garibi Hatao; Can IRDP Do It?', *EPW*, Feb. 7, 1985.

Rau, S.K., 'Strategies for Rural Development', *Kurukshetra*, March 1, 1980.

Reddy, G. Ram, and Hargopal G., 'Rural Development; Implementation is the Crux', *Journal of Social and Economic Studies*, October-December, 1985.

Reserve Bank of India, *All India Rural Debt and Investment Survey, 1961-62*, Bombay, 1965.

———, *All India Debt and Investment Survey, 1971-72*, Vol. 1, Bombay, 1975.

Sadhu and Mahajan, *Technological Change and Agricultural Development in India*, Bombay: Himalaya Publishing House, 1985.

———, 'Economic Efficiency of Agricultural Resources – An Interregional Analysis, *Agricultural Situation in India*, Delhi, 1981.

———, 'Changing Rural Employment Structure and Technology'. *Khadi-gramodyog*, 1983.

Satpathy, K.M., 'IRDP: Monitoring and Evaluation', *Kurukshetra*, December 1, 1981.

Sau, Ranjit, 'Growth, Employment and Removal of Poverty', *EPW*, Aug. 1978.

Sen, A.K., 'Peasant and dualism with or without surplus labour', *Journal of Political Economy*, October 1966.

———, 'Poverty, Inequality and Unemployment; Some conceptual issues in measurement.' *EPW*, August 1973.

Sharma, S.K. and S.C. Malhotra, *Integrated Rural Development*, New Delhi: Abhinav Publication, 1977.

Singh, Bhanwar, *Agrarian Structure Technological Change and Poverty*, New Delhi: Agricole Publishing Academy, 1985.

Singh, H.K. Manmohan, 'Population Pressure and Labour Absorbability in Agriculture and Related Activities; Analysis and Suggestion Based on Field Studies Conducted in Punjab', *EPW*, March 17, 1979.

Singh, Tarlok, Social Science Research and Problems of Poverty, New Delhi: Concept Publishing Company, 1990.

Thimmaiha, G., *Inequality and Poverty*, Bombay: Himalaya Publishing House, 1983.

——— (ed.), *Studies in Rural Development*, Allahabad: Chugh Publications, 1979.

Tiwari, R.N., 'IRDP: Can it improve rural Income distribution', *Kurukshetra*, February 1, 1983.

Tripathi, R.N. *et al.*, *IRDP in South India: An Evaluation*, Hyderabad, National Institute of Rural Development, 1985.

Tripathi, S., The Role of Banks in upliftment of Rural Poor under IRDP, a Project sponsored by B.H.U., Centre for IRDP, Varanasi, 1984.

Vaidyanathan, A., 'Some Aspect of Inequalities in Living Standards in Rural India', in T.N. Srinivasan and P.K. Bardhan (ed.), *Poverty and Income Distribution in India*, 1974.

Verma, S.C., *Millions in Poverty Grip: India's Rural Works Programme*, New Delhi: Kunj Publishing House, 1984.

Vidyarthi, L.P. (ed.), *Rural Development in South Asia*, New Delhi: Concept Publishing Co., 1982.

Visaria, P., 'Poverty and living standard in Asia: An overview of the main results and lesson of selected households surveys', Living Standard Measurement Study Working Paper No. 2, Washington D.C., World Bank.

Wills, I.R., 'Green Revolution and Agricultural Employment and Income in Western U.P.' *EPW*, March 27, 1971.

INDEX